THE GREAT BRITISH QUIZ BOOK

THIS IS A CARLTON BOOK

This edition published in 2013 by
Carlton Books Limited
20 Mortimer Street
London W1T 3JW

ISBN 978-1-78097-432-3

3 5 7 9 10 8 6 4 2

Printed and bound by CPI Group (UK) Ltd, Croydon, CR0 4YY

Some of the material in this book was previously published in
The Biggest Pub Quiz Book Ever!

THE GREAT BRITISH QUIZ BOOK

**Test your knowledge of the United Kingdom's
people, places, customs and culture**

CARLTON
BOOKS

CONTENTS

INTRODUCTION

Welcome to this great quiz book, all about the United Kingdom of Great Britain and Northern Ireland.

This book is filled with questions (and their answers) about all aspects of the UK, from music and theatre to mountains and politics. There are questions for all sorts of abilities and ages, so you should be able to enjoy yourself however old you are and wherever you come from. The people who will be able to answer most questions correctly are those who have lived in the UK for the longest, or maybe those who have studied English and the UK for longest. But don't worry, all the questions are multiple choice so you will never be stuck for an answer!

You could use this book as a quiz by yourself or with friends, as a source of information about all matters pertaining to the UK, or as a fun test of your general knowledge. Whatever you do, try to have fun.

Author's note: you may notice some questions in here that do not exclusively relate to the UK. If that's the case, they will relate to events or cultural references that are deeply ingrained into the UK and its population, so are very relevent in this book.

Have fun, and look out for more books in the series!

QUIZ 1: GEOGRAPHY

1. Which coast of England is Holy Island off?
- [ ] North
- [x] East
- [ ] South
- [ ] West

2. What is a native of Aberdeen called?
- [ ] Aberdonian
- [x] Abridonian
- [ ] Deener
- [ ] Dooner

3. Is London's Docklands, north, south, east or west of the city?
- [ ] North
- [x] East
- [ ] South
- [ ] West

4. The Angel of the North was erected next to which major road?
- [x] A1
- [ ] A4
- [ ] M1
- [ ] M6

5. Which English gorge takes its name from a nearby village famous for its cheese?
- [ ] Caerphilly
- [ ] Chaumes
- [x] Cheddar
- [ ] Stilton

6. Which county has the abbreviation Beds?

☐ Avon
☐ Bedstone
☐ Bradfordshire
☑ Bedfordshire

7. St Anne's lies to the south of which British seaside resort?

☑ Blackpool
☐ Clacton-on-Sea
☐ Lyme Regis
☐ Weston-super-mare

8. Which Royal residence stands by the river Dee?

☑ Balmoral
☐ Buckingham Palace
☐ Checkers
☐ Windsor Castle

9. In which country is the UK's highest mountain?

☐ England
☐ Northern Ireland
☑ Scotland
☐ Wales

10. What sort of an institution in London is Bart's?

☐ Cartoon Museum
☑ Hospital
☐ Old Thespian's Rest Home
☐ Theatre

ANSWERS
1 East. 2 Aberdonian. 3 East. 4 A1. 5 Cheddar. 6 Bedfordshire.
7 Blackpool. 8 Balmoral. 9 Scotland. 10 Hospital.

QUIZ 2: GENERAL

1. On a London Tube map the Central Line is which colour?
- [ ] Dark blue
- [ ] Red
- [ ] Light blue
- [ ] Orange

2. In which Scottish city did you find the Gorbals?
- [ ] Ayr
- [ ] Dundee
- [ ] Edinburgh
- [ ] Glasgow

3. Which motorway links London to Winchester?
- [ ] M1
- [ ] M2
- [ ] M3
- [ ] M4

4. Which Isle off the south coast of England is a county in its own right?
- [ ] Isle of Dogs
- [ ] Isle of Man
- [ ] Isle of Lucy
- [ ] Isle of Wight

5. What is Britain's most southerly country?
- [ ] England
- [ ] Northern Ireland
- [ ] Scotland
- [ ] Wales

6. Norwich is the administrative centre of which county?
- ☐ Cambridgeshire
- ☐ Norwichfolk
- ☐ Norfolk
- ☐ Suffolk

7. In which city did the National Trust buy the childhood home of Paul McCartney?
- ☐ Blackpool
- ☐ Ellesmere Port
- ☐ Liverpool
- ☐ Manchester

8. Which motorway runs almost parallel to the A4?
- ☐ A34
- ☐ A2B
- ☐ B4
- ☐ M4

9. With which profession is London's Harley Street associated?
- ☐ Engineering
- ☐ Medical
- ☐ Publishing
- ☐ Veterinarian

10. What is Britain's largest international airport?
- ☐ Gatwick
- ☐ Heathrow
- ☐ London City
- ☐ Southend

ANSWERS

1 Red. 2 Glasgow. 3 M3. 4 Isle of Wight. 5 England. 6 Norfolk.
7 Liverpool. 8 M4. 9 Medical profession. 10 Heathrow.

11

QUIZ 3: AROUND

1. In which county is Land's End?
- [ ] Avon
- [ ] Cornwall
- [ ] Devon
- [ ] Somerset

2. What colour are most London buses?
- [ ] Black
- [ ] Green
- [ ] Pink
- [ ] Red

3. Which motorway goes from Lancashire to Yorkshire east to west?
- [ ] M1
- [ ] M20
- [ ] M4
- [ ] M62

4. What is the background colour of road signs to tourist sites?
- [ ] Black
- [ ] Brown
- [ ] Blue
- [ ] Pink

5. In which part of the UK is "Land of My Fathers" a traditional song?
- [ ] England
- [ ] Northern Ireland
- [ ] Scotland
- [ ] Wales

THE U.K.

6. Winchester is the adminstrative seat of which county?
- [ ] Berkshire
- [ ] Cheshire
- [ ] Hampshire
- [ ] Winshire

7. Aston University is in which Midlands city?
- [ ] Birmingham
- [ ] Coventry
- [ ] Royal Leamington Spa
- [ ] Rugby

8. Most of the Lake District is in which county?
- [ ] Cumbria
- [ ] Lancashire
- [ ] Merseyside
- [ ] North Yorkshire

9. What red flower does Lancs have?
- [ ] Carnation
- [ ] Peony
- [ ] Poppy
- [ ] Rose

10. In which city is the Barbican Centre?
- [ ] Bristol
- [ ] Barbiton
- [ ] Cardiff
- [ ] London

———————————————————————————— ANSWERS
7 Birmingham. 8 Cumbria. 9 Rose. 10 London.
1 Cornwall. 2 Red. 3 M62. 4 Brown. 5 Wales. 6 Hampshire.

13

QUIZ 4: POP MUSIC

1. Which Spice Girl advertised Milky Bars as a child?
- ☐ Baby
- ☐ Posh
- ☐ Nice
- ☐ Scary

2. How old was Billie Piper when she first went to No. 1?
- ☐ 5
- ☐ 10
- ☐ 15
- ☐ 20

3. What is the first name of the Welsh singer from Catatonia?
- ☐ Myfanwy
- ☐ Nerys
- ☐ Nesta
- ☐ Rhiannon

4. Which 60s singer's first hit was written by the Rolling Stones?
- ☐ Cilla Black
- ☐ Petula Clark
- ☐ Kiki Dee
- ☐ Marianne Faithfull

5. Heather Small found fame with which band?
- ☐ MTGG
- ☐ M People
- ☐ N Dubz
- ☐ N People

6. In which body part do Scary Spice and Princess Anne's daughter both have a stud?

- [ ] Belly button
- [ ] Cheek
- [ ] Nose
- [ ] Tongue

7. Which 60s singer hosted "Surprise Surprise"?

- [ ] Cilla Black
- [ ] Marianne Faithfull
- [ ] Lulu
- [ ] Helen Shapiro

8. Who sang about 'Baboushka' and 'Wuthering Heights'?

- [ ] Natasha Bedingfield
- [ ] Kate Bush
- [ ] Rosie Cheeks
- [ ] Cherie Tree

9. In which decade did Bananarama have their first hit?

- [ ] 1970s
- [ ] 1980s
- [ ] 1990s
- [ ] 2000s

10. Which of the following is *not* a British singer?

- [ ] Kiki Dee
- [ ] Bonny St Claire
- [ ] Tammy St John
- [ ] Twinkle

ANSWERS

1 Emma (Baby Spice). 2 15. 3 Nerys. 4 Marianne Faithfull. 5 M People. 6 Tongue. 7 Cilla Black. 8 Kate Bush. 9 1980s. 10 Bonny St Claire.

15

QUIZ 5: ROYALS

1. How many daughters does Queen Elizabeth II have??
- [ ] 1
- [ ] 2
- [ ] 3
- [ ] 4

2. Who is the father of Princes William and Harry?
- [ ] Prince Albert
- [ ] Prince Charles
- [ ] Prince Michael
- [ ] Prince Philip

3. What title did Camilla Parker Bowles use after she married Prince Charles?
- [ ] Duchess
- [ ] Frau
- [ ] Lady
- [ ] Princess

4. In which country did Princess Diana tragically meet her death?
- [ ] France
- [ ] Ireland
- [ ] Luxembourg
- [ ] Monaco

5. What did Prince Harry join after his gap year?
- [ ] Army
- [ ] Navy
- [ ] Royal Marines
- [ ] UKIP

6. What is the Queen's residence in Scotland called?

☐ Balmoonie
☐ Balmoral
☐ Chequers
☐ Windsor Castle

7. Which Prince is Duke of Edinburgh?

☐ Albert
☐ Charles
☐ Michael
☐ Philip

8. Which Prince was a helicopter pilot in the Falklands War?

☐ Andrew
☐ Charles
☐ Eric
☐ Philip

9. Who is the Princess Royal?

☐ Anne
☐ Camilla
☐ Eugenie
☐ Stephanie

10. How many children does the Duchess of Cornwall have??

☐ 1
☐ 2
☐ 3
☐ 4

ANSWERS

1 One. 2 Prince Charles. 3 Duchess. 4 France. 5 Army.
6 Balmoral. 7 Philip. 8 Andrew. 9 Anne. 10 Two.

17

QUIZ 6: ENGLAND

1. The Severn, the Trent and the Ouse are all what?
- [ ] Counties
- [ ] Islands
- [ ] Mountains
- [ ] Rivers

2. In which county are all ten of England's highest peaks?
- [ ] Cumbria
- [ ] Essex
- [ ] Scotland
- [ ] Yorkshire

3. Which is the second largest city in England?
- [ ] Birmingham
- [ ] Brighton
- [ ] Manchester
- [ ] York

4. Which London station was named after a long-reigning Queen?
- [ ] Liverpool Street
- [ ] Pimlico
- [ ] St Pancras
- [ ] Victoria

5. In which county are the seaside resorts of Clacton and Southend?
- [ ] Cambridgeshire
- [ ] Essex
- [ ] Lancashire
- [ ] Suffolk

6. Leeds Castle is in Kent. Where is Leeds?

- ☐ Cumbria
- ☐ Essex
- ☐ Scotland
- ☐ Yorkshire

7. Which resort is famous for its Tower and its Golden Mile?

- ☐ Blackpool
- ☐ Clacton-on-Sea
- ☐ Lyme Regis
- ☐ Weston-super-mare

8. What might you see at Regent's Park, Chester and Whipsnade?

- ☐ Amusement park
- ☐ Safari park
- ☐ Statues of Elvis
- ☐ Zoo

9. What is the name of the famous cathedral in York?

- ☐ George
- ☐ The Minster
- ☐ The Minister
- ☐ The Yorker

10. Which is the largest island in England?

- ☐ Isle of Lucy
- ☐ Isle of Man
- ☐ Isle of White
- ☐ Isle of Wight

ANSWERS

1 Rivers. 2 Cumbria. 3 Birmingham. 4 Victoria. 5 Essex.
6 Yorkshire. 7 Blackpool. 8 Zoo. 9 The Minster. 10 Isle of Wight.

19

QUIZ 7: MUSICALS

1. Michael Crawford starred in the musical about "The Woman" in which colour?

- ☐ Betty
- ☐ Black
- ☐ Green
- ☐ White

2. Who wrote the long-running play "The Mousetrap"?

- ☐ Danny Boyle
- ☐ Agatha Christie
- ☐ Noel Coward
- ☐ William Shakespeare

3. Complete the title of the comedy: "No Sex Please _____"?

- ☐ We're brattish
- ☐ We're British
- ☐ We're French
- ☐ We're frigid

4. In "Starlight Express" what did performers wear on their feet?

- ☐ Banana skins
- ☐ Hobnailed boots
- ☐ Ice skates
- ☐ Roller skates

5. What was Jesus Christ according to Tim Rice and Andrew Lloyd Webber?

- ☐ Crucified
- ☐ Superb
- ☐ Superman
- ☐ Superstar

AND THEATRE

6. According to the comedy, There's a what in My Soup?
- ☐ Fly
- ☐ Girl
- ☐ Hair
- ☐ Waitor

7. Which London theatre's motto was, "We never closed"?
- ☐ The Always Open
- ☐ Catamaran
- ☐ Moulin
- ☐ Windmill

8. Who wrote the music in the comic operas for which Gilbert wrote the words?
- ☐ Gecko
- ☐ George
- ☐ Hammerstein
- ☐ Sullivan

9. What do the initials RSC stand for?
- ☐ Real Super Club
- ☐ Regal Shakespeare Company
- ☐ Royal Shakespeare Club
- ☐ Royal Shakespeare Company

10. Which musical is based on T. S. Eliot's poems?
- ☐ Cats
- ☐ Dogs
- ☐ Hair
- ☐ Mama Mia

ANSWERS

1 White. 2 Agatha Christie. 3 We're British. 4 Skates. 5 Superstar. 6 Girl. 7 The Windmill. 8 Sullivan. 9 Royal Shakespeare Company. 10 Cats.

21

QUIZ 8: 1960s TV

1. Which soap, which started in 1960, tells of life in Weatherfield?
- [ ] Brookside
- [ ] Coronation Street
- [ ] Eastenders
- [ ] Neighbours

2. Which Cars were at the heart of a long-running police drama series?
- [ ] A to Z cars
- [ ] Police cars
- [ ] Star cars
- [ ] Z cars

3. Which family Saga spanned the Victorian and Edwardian eras?
- [ ] The Archers
- [ ] Forsyte Saga
- [ ] The Forsythe Saga
- [ ] Upstairs Downstairs

4. Which university quiz was hosted by Bamber Gascoigne?
- [ ] University Challenge
- [ ] University Wipeout
- [ ] The Weakest Link
- [ ] The Weakest University

5. What did you Thank in the ITV Saturday-evening pop show?
- [ ] Simon Cowell
- [ ] God
- [ ] Your Lucky Stars
- [ ] Your Music Collection

6. Which Doctor arrived on our screens in the Tardis in 1963?

- ☐ Brown
- ☐ Finlay
- ☐ Love
- ☐ Who

7. Whose Casebook was based in a Scottish village surgery?

- ☐ Dr Finlay
- ☐ Dr Who
- ☐ Ironside
- ☐ Monarch of the Glen

8. Which Birds were flatmates in Liverpool?

- ☐ Busby Babes
- ☐ Gorgeous
- ☐ Liver Birds
- ☐ Manchester Birds

9. Which show began broadcasting highlights of the day's football?

- ☐ Football Italia
- ☐ The Match
- ☐ Match of the Day
- ☐ Match Play

10. What was the first name of sci-fi adventurer Adamant?

- ☐ Arthur
- ☐ Adam
- ☐ Adamski
- ☐ Johan

1 Coronation Street. 2 Cars. 3 Forsyte Saga. 4 University Challenge. 5 Your Lucky Stars. 6 Dr Who. 7 Dr Finlay. 8 Liver Birds. 9 Match of the Day. 10 Adam.

23

QUIZ 9: SCOTLAND

1. Dundee is on which coast of Scotland?
- ☐ North
- ☐ East
- ☐ South
- ☐ West

2. Which is the most northerly point on the British mainland?
- ☐ John Oats
- ☐ John O'Groats
- ☐ Land's End
- ☐ Stormont

3. Which city is Scotland's capital?
- ☐ Dundee
- ☐ Edinburgh
- ☐ Glasgow
- ☐ Motherwell

4. Are Scottish banknotes legal tender in England?
- ☐ Yes
- ☐ No
- ☐ Only on weekdays
- ☐ Only for exchange in banks

5. Who built a wall to divide Scotland from England?
- ☐ Adrian
- ☐ King Arthur
- ☐ Caesar
- ☐ Hadrian

6. Where is the Royal and Ancient Golf Club?
- [ ] St Alfreds
- [ ] Edinburgh
- [ ] Glasgow
- [ ] St Andrews

7. The name of which Scottish product means "water of life"?
- [ ] Football
- [ ] Haggis
- [ ] Spring water
- [ ] Whisky

8. Where is the Queen's Scottish residence?
- [ ] Balmoral
- [ ] Checkers
- [ ] Buckingham Palace
- [ ] Windsor Castle

9. What is the name of the Games held at Braemar?
- [ ] Gaelic Games
- [ ] Highland Games
- [ ] Lowland Games
- [ ] Scottish Games

10. Which sport is Aviemore particularly famous for?
- [ ] Climbing
- [ ] Golf
- [ ] Sailing
- [ ] Skiing

ANSWERS

1 East. 2 John o' Groat's. 3 Edinburgh. 4 Yes. 5 Hadrian. 6 St Andrews. 7 Whisky. 8 Balmoral. 9 Highland Games. 10 Skiing.

QUIZ 10: CRICKET

1. Which international teams contest the Ashes?

☐ Australia and New Zealand
☐ Australia and England
☐ England and New Zealand
☐ England and Scotland

2. In which city is the ground Old Trafford?

☐ Liverpool
☐ London
☐ Manchester
☐ Nottingham

3. In LBW what does the B stand for?

☐ By
☐ Best
☐ Before
☐ Bloody

4. Which bowler Dominic took a Test hat-trick in 1995?

☐ Cork
☐ Monahan
☐ Stamp
☐ York

5. Which cricketer was voted BBC Sports Personality for 2005?

☐ Andrew Flintoff
☐ Graham Gooch
☐ Ricky Ponting
☐ Michael Vaughn

6. Which wicket keeper shares his name with a breed of dog?

☐ Dachsund

☐ Rolf

☐ Russell

☐ St Bernard

7. The Nursery End, the Pavilion End and St John's Wood Road are all linked with which ground?

☐ Lords

☐ Old Trafford

☐ The Oval

☐ Trent Bridge

8. Which former England batsman Derek was known as "Rags"?

☐ Raggin

☐ Randall

☐ Rawlings

☐ Wright

9. Which patriotic song was adopted by England in the 2005 Ashes?

☐ God Save The Queen

☐ Jerusalem

☐ Rule Britannia

☐ Swing Low Sweet Chariot

10. Robin Smith is an international for which country?

☐ Scotland

☐ Wales

☐ England

☐ Northern Ireland

ANSWERS

1 Australia and England. 2 Manchester. 3 Before. 4 Cork. 5 Andrew Flintoff. 6 Jack Russell. 7 Lord's. 8 Randall. 9 Jerusalem. 10 England.

27

QUIZ 11: MIXTURE

1. If it rains on St Swithin's Day, how many more days is it supposed to rain?
- [ ] 7
- [ ] 30
- [ ] 40
- [ ] 364

2. By which name of one word is Katie Price better known?
- [ ] Caprice
- [ ] Jordan
- [ ] Kylie
- [ ] Pricey

3. The album "Tissues and Issues" was a success for which star?
- [ ] Adele
- [ ] Bruno Mars
- [ ] Charlotte Church
- [ ] Jessie J

4. What is a low, shallow basket used by gardeners called?
- [ ] Basket
- [ ] Tasket
- [ ] Trug
- [ ] Tug

5. In "David Copperfield" what was the surname of Uriah?
- [ ] Cheap
- [ ] Dickens
- [ ] Heap
- [ ] Neep

6. What is the first name of the main detective in "A Touch of Frost"?

☐ Ben
☐ David
☐ Dick
☐ Jack

7. In which month is Remembrance Day?

☐ January
☐ March
☐ November
☐ December

8. Which TV drama was set in Glenbogle?

☐ The Crow Road
☐ Dr Finlay's Casebook
☐ Monarch of the Glen
☐ Take The High Road

9. What are the initials of "Lady Chatterley" author Lawrence?

☐ D. H.
☐ H. D.
☐ H. P.
☐ R. H.

10. What type of dancing is associated with Margot Fonteyn?

☐ Ballet
☐ Charleston
☐ Modern
☐ Tap

ANSWERS

1 40. 2 Jordan. 3 Charlotte Church. 4 Trug. 5 Heap. 6 Jack. 7 November. 8 Monarch of the Glen. 9 D. H. 10 Ballet.

29

QUIZ 12: 1970S MUSIC

1. Which Brotherhood had a Eurovision winner in 1976?

☐ Brotherhood of Brothers
☐ Brotherhood of Man
☐ Brotherhood of Nan
☐ Brotherhood of Woman

2. Peters and who said "Welcome Home" in 1973?

☐ Arno
☐ Jackson
☐ Lee
☐ Smee

3. Which Gary was Leader of the Gang?

☐ Glitter
☐ Lineker
☐ Silver
☐ Sobers

4. Which City Rollers had a hit with "Bye Bye Baby"?

☐ Bay
☐ London
☐ Windy
☐ York

5. A "Ballroom Blitz" came from which sugary-sounding group?

☐ Bonbons
☐ The Jam
☐ Sugarpops
☐ Sweet

6. What had the T originally stood for in T Rex?

☐ Terrible
☐ Triumph
☐ Trousers
☐ Tyrannosaurus

7. Which group sang "Weer All Crazee Now"?

☐ The Clash
☐ Iron Maiden
☐ Slade
☐ Wizzard

8. Who sang "Do Ya Think I'm Sexy"?

☐ Jane Birkin
☐ David Bowie
☐ Joe Cocker
☐ Rod Stewart

9. Who first sang with Elton John on "Don't Go Breaking My Heart"?

☐ Kiki Dee
☐ Marcella Detroit
☐ George Michael
☐ RuPaul

10. "Bohemian Rhapsody" was recorded by which group?

☐ Led Zeppelin
☐ Level 42
☐ Queen
☐ The Rolling Stones

ANSWERS

6 Tyrannosaurus. 7 Slade. 8 Rod Stewart. 9 Kiki Dee. 10 Queen.
1 The Brotherhood of Man. 2 Lee. 3 Glitter. 4 Bay. 5 Sweet.

31

QUIZ 13: FOOD

1. What is the main ingredient in an omelette?
- ☐ Eggs
- ☐ Flour
- ☐ Milk
- ☐ Water

2. Which animal does venison come from?
- ☐ Chicken
- ☐ Deer
- ☐ Goat
- ☐ Sheep

3. Which garden herb is made into a sauce often eaten with lamb?
- ☐ Cranberry
- ☐ Mint
- ☐ Rosemary
- ☐ Thyme

4. In which country did the word biscuit originate?
- ☐ England
- ☐ France
- ☐ Ireland
- ☐ USA

5. What is traditionally eaten on Shrove Tuesday?
- ☐ Bananas
- ☐ Cheese
- ☐ Pancakes
- ☐ Sweets

6. What is the British term for French fries?
- ☐ Bangers
- ☐ Chips
- ☐ Freedom Fries
- ☐ Spuds

7. What is a slice of bacon called?
- ☐ Chop
- ☐ Rasher
- ☐ Rind
- ☐ Scalp

8. Which edible sugary substance do bees make?
- ☐ Fudge
- ☐ Golden syrup
- ☐ Honey
- ☐ Sugar

9. What is done to a herring to make it into a kipper?
- ☐ Battered
- ☐ Gutted
- ☐ Peeled
- ☐ Smoked

10. Which vegetable can be King Edward or Desirée?
- ☐ Bean
- ☐ Carrot
- ☐ Pea
- ☐ Potato

ANSWERS

1 Eggs. 2 Deer. 3 Mint. 4 France. 5 Pancakes. 6 Chips. 7 Rasher. 8 Honey. 9 Smoked. 10 Potato.

QUIZ 14: 1970s TV

1. Which Irish comedian held a cigarette, sat on a bar stool and chatted?
- ☐ Dave Allen
- ☐ Ardle O'Hanlan
- ☐ Graham Norton
- ☐ Father Ted

2. What was the profession of the Angels?
- ☐ Crime fighters
- ☐ Nurses
- ☐ Nuns
- ☐ Soldiers

3. Which poetess Pam won "Opportunity Knocks" in 1975?
- ☐ Ayres
- ☐ Polythene
- ☐ Smith
- ☐ Stephenson

4. The Duchess of which street was part of a drama series?
- ☐ Duke Street
- ☐ High Street
- ☐ Old Street
- ☐ York Street

5. Which king and son of Queen Victoria was the subject of a TV serial?
- ☐ Charles
- ☐ Edward
- ☐ Philip
- ☐ Victor

6. Which Tudor queen was played by Glenda Jackson?
- [ ] Anne
- [ ] Elizabeth I
- [ ] Elizabeth II
- [ ] Victoria

7. The Fall and Rise of who was played by Leonard Rossiter?
- [ ] George Best
- [ ] Colonel Blimp
- [ ] Reginald Perrin
- [ ] Leonard Rossiter

8. What was the first name of Basil Fawlty's wife?
- [ ] Cyris
- [ ] Jane
- [ ] Sheila
- [ ] Sybil

9. How were Bill Oddie, Tim Brooke-Taylor and Graeme Garden known?
- [ ] The Baddies
- [ ] The Goodies
- [ ] The Loonies
- [ ] Three of a kind

10. Which children's series told of life in a London comprehensive?
- [ ] Blue Peter
- [ ] Byker Grove
- [ ] Dangermouse
- [ ] Grange Hill

ANSWERS

1 Dave Allen. 2 Nurses. 3 Ayres. 4 Duke Street. 5 Edward VII. 6 Elizabeth I. 7 Reginald Perrin. 8 Sybil. 9 The Goodies. 10 Grange Hill.

35

QUIZ 15: WALES

1. What is Wales' highest mountain?
☐ Ben Doon
☐ Ben Nevis
☐ Pen Y Fan
☐ Snowdon

2. Which Welshman wrote "Portrait of the Artist as a Young Dog"?
☐ Bob Dylan
☐ Dylan Fisher
☐ Dylan Thomas
☐ John Thomas

3. Which Sea is to the north of Wales?
☐ English Channel
☐ Irish Sea
☐ North Sea
☐ Welsh Sea

4. What are the Brecon Beacons?
☐ Brothers
☐ Drinks
☐ Fires
☐ Mountains

5. Which island lies off the north west coast of Wales?
☐ Anglsey
☐ Cardiff
☐ Isle of Man
☐ Isle of Wight

6. Which spring flower is a Welsh emblem?

- ☐ Bluebell
- ☐ Daffodil
- ☐ Snowdrop
- ☐ Violet

7. What is the capital of Wales?

- ☐ Cardiff
- ☐ Newport
- ☐ Pontefract
- ☐ Swansea

8. Which Channel is to the south of Wales?

- ☐ Bristol Channel
- ☐ Cornish Channel
- ☐ Swansea Channel
- ☐ Welsh Channel

9. Where is Caernarvon Castle in Wales?

- ☐ North
- ☐ South
- ☐ East
- ☐ West

10. Caerphilly is a town and also what type of food?

- ☐ Cabbage
- ☐ Cheese
- ☐ Leek
- ☐ Mushroom

ANSWERS

1 Snowdon. 2 Dylan Thomas. 3 Irish Sea. 4 Mountains. 5 Anglesey.
6 Daffodil. 7 Cardiff. 8 Bristol Channel. 9 North. 10 Cheese.

37

QUIZ 17: SOAPS

1. Which father and son both came to a sticky end in "EastEnders" in 2005?

☐ Ali & Simon
☐ Arthur & Ian
☐ Den & Dennis
☐ Grant & Phil

2. What was Sharon's surname after she married Dennis?

☐ Clarke
☐ Fowler
☐ Rickman
☐ Wise

3. Who is the Street's repetitive butcher?

☐ Frank Butcher
☐ Fred Bolton
☐ Fred Burgess
☐ Fred Elliott

4. In which soap did Dave Glover perish in a fire?

☐ Brookside
☐ Coronation Street
☐ Crossroads
☐ Emmerdale

5. Which "Coronation Street" MacDonald twin went to prison?

☐ Andy
☐ Jim
☐ Steve
☐ Stewart

6. Sunita of "Coronation Street" played who in "Dinnerladies"?

☐ Anita
☐ Alison
☐ Neeta
☐ Nettie

7. What is Dr Brendan McGuire's nickname in "Doctors"?

☐ Brenda
☐ Doc
☐ Mac
☐ Macca

8. Who was a vet in "All Creatures Great and Small" and a doctor in "Doctors"?

☐ Tim Christopher
☐ Peter Davison
☐ Robert Hardy
☐ Christopher Timothy

9. Which brothers returned to "EastEnders" in 2005?

☐ Cotton
☐ Fowler
☐ Hall
☐ Mitchell

10. In "Neighbours" what was the surname of Scott, Paul, Lucy and Julie?

☐ Bishop
☐ Daniels
☐ Mitchell
☐ Robinson

ANSWERS

1 Den & Dennis. 2 Rickman. 3 Fred Elliott. 4 "Emmerdale". 5 Steve. 6 Anita. 7 Mac. 8 Christopher Timothy. 9 Mitchells. 10 Robinson.

39

QUIZ 18: THE UK

1. Glasgow is the administrative centre of which Scottish region?
- ☐ Borders
- ☐ Fife
- ☐ Grampian
- ☐ Strathclyde

2. Which is further north, Liverpool or Leeds?
- ☐ Grimsby
- ☐ Leeds
- ☐ Liverpool
- ☐ Stoke on Trent

3. What before the 1996 reorganization was the only Welsh county to begin with C?
- ☐ Camarthen
- ☐ Cardiff
- ☐ Cleves
- ☐ Clwyd

4. Which motorway would you travel on from London to Leeds?
- ☐ A1
- ☐ A4
- ☐ M1
- ☐ M6

5. How is the Welsh island Ynys Mon also known?
- ☐ Anglesey
- ☐ Grassholm
- ☐ Isle of Man
- ☐ Skomer

6. In which part of the UK is Newry?
- ☐ England
- ☐ Northern Ireland
- ☐ Scotland
- ☐ Wales

7. How many counties have a border with Cornwall?
- ☐ 1
- ☐ 2
- ☐ 3
- ☐ 4

8. In which District are Ullswater and Bassenthwaite?
- ☐ Lakeland
- ☐ Lake District
- ☐ Land O'Lakes
- ☐ Loch District

9. Which resort beginning with S lies between Whitby and Bridlington?
- ☐ Scarborough
- ☐ Skegness
- ☐ Sleights
- ☐ Southend

10. In which country is Prestwick Airport?
- ☐ England
- ☐ Northern Ireland
- ☐ Scotland
- ☐ Wales

ANSWERS

Strathclyde. 2 Leeds. 3 Clwyd. 4 M1. 5 Anglesey. 6 Northern Ireland. 7 One – Devon. 8 Lake District. 9 Scarborough. 10 Scotland.

41

QUIZ 19: FOOTBALL

1. At which club were Niall Quinn & Kevin Phillips strikers?
- [ ] Liverpool
- [ ] Newcastle United
- [ ] Southampton
- [ ] Sunderland

2. Who scored England's goal against Brazil in the 2002 World Cup?
- [ ] Tony Adams
- [ ] John Barnes
- [ ] David Beckham
- [ ] Michael Owen

3. Gilberto Silva won the World Cup with which country?
- [ ] Argentina
- [ ] Brazil
- [ ] Italy
- [ ] Uruguay

4. Who was Arsenal's regular keeper in the 1970–71 double season?
- [ ] George Graham
- [ ] David Seaman
- [ ] Bob Wilson
- [ ] Rob Wilson

5. Which player was nicknamed "The Divine Ponytail"?
- [ ] Roberto Baggio
- [ ] Perluigi Collina
- [ ] Ruud Gullit
- [ ] Paolo Maldini

6. Which was the first English club to instal an artificial pitch?
- [ ] Arsenal
- [ ] Manchster United
- [ ] QPR
- [ ] Stoke City

7. Who was Blackburn's benefactor of the 90s?
- [ ] Roman Abramovic
- [ ] Jack Black
- [ ] Jack Wales
- [ ] Jack Walker

8. Robins, Valiants and Addicks are all nicknames of which team?
- [ ] Aston Villa
- [ ] Bristol City
- [ ] Bristol Rovers
- [ ] Charlton

9. Who took Wigan into the Premiership for the first time?
- [ ] Paul Jewell
- [ ] Kevin Keegan
- [ ] Roberto Martinez
- [ ] Stuart Pearce

10. What colour are Wales international home shirts?
- [ ] Blue
- [ ] Red
- [ ] White
- [ ] Yellow

ANSWERS

1 Sunderland. 2 Michael Owen. 3 Brazil. 4 Bob Wilson. 5 Roberto Baggio. 6 QPR.
7 Jack Walker. 8 Charlton. 9 Paul Jewell. 10 Yellow.

43

QUIZ 16: 1980S TV

1. Which series was about Yorkshire vet James Herriot?

☐ All Creatures Great and Small
☐ Animal Hospital
☐ It's A Vet's Life
☐ Some Mothers Do 'Ave 'Em

2. In which series would you find the Fallen Madonna with the Big Boobies?

☐ Allo Allo
☐ Dad's Army
☐ It Ain't Alf Hot Mum
☐ Top of the Pops

3. On which island was "Bergerac" set?

☐ Alderney
☐ Guernesey
☐ Jersey
☐ Sark

4. Which programme gave the catchphrase "Gissa job"?

☐ Boys from the Blackstuff
☐ Bread
☐ Cracker
☐ Jobsearch

5. What was Revisited in the series with Jeremy Irons?

☐ Brideshead
☐ Eton
☐ Oxford
☐ Sexuality

6. What was Jeremy Beadle Game for?

- ☐ A Camera
- ☐ A Clue
- ☐ A Laugh
- ☐ A Wedding

7. Which Russell was astrologer on "Breakfast Time"?

- ☐ Beattie
- ☐ Brand
- ☐ Crow
- ☐ Grant

8. Which religious programme did Harry Secombe start to present?

- ☐ Highway
- ☐ God's Way
- ☐ Morning Worship
- ☐ Songs of Praise

9. What was the Hitch Hiker's Guide to?

- ☐ England
- ☐ The Galaxy
- ☐ The Universe
- ☐ Wales

10. What was being built in the yards in "Howard's Way"?

- ☐ Boats
- ☐ Cameras
- ☐ Cars
- ☐ Tube trains

ANSWERS

1 All Creatures Great and Small. 2 Allo Allo. 3 Jersey. 4 Boys from the Blackstuff.
5 Brideshead. 6. A Laugh. 7 Grant. 8 Highway 9 The Galaxy. 10 Boats.

45

QUIZ 20: ROYALTY

1. In which decade did Prince Charles marry Lady Diana Spencer?
- ☐ 1990s
- ☐ 1980s
- ☐ 1970s
- ☐ 1960s

2. In 2002 the Queen celebrated how many years as monarch?
- ☐ 50
- ☐ 25
- ☐ 55
- ☐ 75

3. Prince Michael's title is of which county?
- ☐ Cornwall
- ☐ Essex
- ☐ Kent
- ☐ Suffolk

4. Who is the elder of Prince Andrew's daughters?
- ☐ Beatrice
- ☐ Daphne
- ☐ Eugenie
- ☐ Henrietta

5. What is Princess Anne's son's first name?
- ☐ Charles
- ☐ Carlos
- ☐ Peter
- ☐ Philip

6. Which royal title do Princess Anne's children have?

- ☐ Prince/Princess of Liverpool
- ☐ Their Royal Highnesses
- ☐ Princes/Princesses Royal
- ☐ None

7. What was the occupation of the late Princess Margaret's first husband?

- ☐ Barber
- ☐ Barrister
- ☐ Photographer
- ☐ Printer

8. What was the name of the king who abdicated in 1936?

- ☐ Charles
- ☐ Edward
- ☐ Edwin
- ☐ Eric

9. What was the surname of the woman he married a year later?

- ☐ Simpkins
- ☐ Simpson
- ☐ Smith
- ☐ Wales

10. What was the name of the first monarch of the 20th century?

- ☐ Charles
- ☐ Edward
- ☐ Elizabeth
- ☐ Victoria

ANSWERS

1 1980s. 2 Fifty. 3 Kent. 4 Beatrice. 5 Peter. 6 None. 7 Photographer. 8 Edward (VIII). 9 Simpson. 10 Victoria.

47

QUIZ 21: THE 1950s

1. In 1959, which party was elected for the third time in a row in Britain?
- [ ] Conservative
- [ ] Labour
- [ ] Liberal
- [ ] SDP

2. Which Donald set a world water speed record?
- [ ] Campbell
- [ ] Canard
- [ ] Draper
- [ ] Smith

3. Which monarch died at Sandringham in 1952?
- [ ] Edward VII
- [ ] George V
- [ ] George VI
- [ ] Victoria

4. "The Mousetrap" opened its London run; who wrote it?
- [ ] Agatha Christie
- [ ] Noel Coward
- [ ] Andrew Lloyd Weber
- [ ] Cameron Mackintosh

5. The first of which contest was won by a woman from Sweden in 1951?
- [ ] Eurovision
- [ ] Juke Box Jury
- [ ] Miss World
- [ ] Opportunity Knocks

6. Which American evangelist Billy led a London crusade?

- [ ] Bunter
- [ ] Crystal
- [ ] Graham
- [ ] Smart

7. Which 77-year-old was returned as British Prime Minister?

- [ ] Neville Chamberlin
- [ ] Winston Churchill
- [ ] Norman Tebbit
- [ ] Margaret Thatcher

8. Which Sir Gordon won the Derby for the first time?

- [ ] Rich
- [ ] Richards
- [ ] Richmond
- [ ] Wright

9. Which Anthony became British Prime Minister in the 50s?

- [ ] Blunt
- [ ] Churchill
- [ ] Eden
- [ ] Stamp

10. "Lord of the Flies" was written by which author William?

- [ ] Ellis
- [ ] Golding
- [ ] Hague
- [ ] Smith

ANSWERS

1 Conservative. 2 Campbell. 3 George VI. 4 Agatha Christie. 5 Miss World. 6 Graham.
7 Winston Churchill. 8 Richards. 9 Eden. 10 Golding.

QUIZ 22: BOOKS

1. Charles Dodgson wrote his classic children's story under what name?
- [ ] Lewis Carroll
- [ ] Charlie
- [ ] Charles Dickens
- [ ] Charles M. Schultz

2. Which Frederick wrote "The Day of the Jackal"?
- [ ] M. Cain
- [ ] Flintoff
- [ ] Forsythe
- [ ] Reynolds

3. Fitzwilliam Darcy appears in which novel?
- [ ] Jane Eyre
- [ ] Pride and Prejudice
- [ ] Roots
- [ ] Sense and Sensibility

4. Whom did Bertie Wooster have as his manservant?
- [ ] Butler
- [ ] Jeeves
- [ ] Sebastien
- [ ] Smythe

5. Which Irving Welsh novel was about Scottish heroin addicts?
- [ ] The Acid House
- [ ] Filth
- [ ] Marabou Stork Nightmares
- [ ] Trainspotting

6. Which county in England did Laurie Lee come from?

- ☐ Cheshire
- ☐ Devon
- ☐ Gloucestershire
- ☐ Somerset

7. Which Arthur wrote the children's classic "Swallows and Amazons"?

- ☐ Dickens
- ☐ Rackham
- ☐ Ransome
- ☐ Smith

8. Which James became Britain's most read vet?

- ☐ Caan
- ☐ Herriot
- ☐ Jeffers
- ☐ Joyce

9. Who created Thomas the Tank Engine?

- ☐ Rev. Awdry
- ☐ Rev. James Awston
- ☐ Enid Blyton
- ☐ Ringo Starr

10. What was the first name of the girl who went to live at Green Gables?

- ☐ Anne
- ☐ Annie
- ☐ Daphne
- ☐ Hermione

ANSWERS

1 Lewis Carroll. 2 Forsyth. 3 Pride and Prejudice. 4 Jeeves. 5 Trainspotting.
6 Gloucestershire. 7 Rackham. 8 Herriot. 9 Rev. Awdry. 10 Anne.

QUIZ 23: THE 1960S

1. Who made the "wind of change" speech?
- [ ] Winston Churchill
- [ ] Harold Macmillan
- [ ] Norman Tebbit
- [ ] Margaret Thatcher

2. George Cohen was a member of the world's winners at which sport?
- [ ] Athletics
- [ ] Cricket
- [ ] Football
- [ ] Tennis

3. Which call-girl Christine was involved in a government scandal?
- [ ] Keeler
- [ ] O'Connor
- [ ] Smith
- [ ] Wheeler

4. Which future Princess of Wales was born in the 60s?
- [ ] Anne
- [ ] Camilla
- [ ] Diana
- [ ] Michael

5. Who played piano while Peter Cook sang?
- [ ] Dave Allen
- [ ] John Cleese
- [ ] Dudley Moore
- [ ] Richard Stillgoe

10 Beeching.

6. Whom did Anthony Armstrong-Jones marry in 1960?

☐ Princess Anne
☐ Princess Margaret
☐ Margaret Rutherford
☐ Mararet Thatcher

7. How did the English comic Tony Hancock die?

☐ Car accident
☐ Heart attack
☐ Murdered
☐ Suicide

8. What does the H stand for in D. H. Lawrence?

☐ Henry
☐ Harry
☐ Herbert
☐ Hiram

9. Bob Dylan starred at a 1969 rock Festival on which British isle?

☐ Anglesey
☐ Canvey Island
☐ Isle of Man
☐ Isle of Wight

10. Which doctor's report led to the cutting of the railway network?

☐ Beachcroft
☐ Beeching
☐ Finlay
☐ Leary

ANSWERS
1 Harold Macmillan. 2 Football. 3 Keeler. 4 Lady Diana Spencer. 5 Dudley Moore. 6 Princess Margaret. 7 Committed suicide. 8 Herbert. 9 Isle of Wight.

53

QUIZ 24: MEDIA

1. Which British daily paper was founded in the 1960s?
- ☐ Evening Gazette
- ☐ Financial Times
- ☐ The Star
- ☐ The Sun

2. Which independent TV company serves East Anglia?
- ☐ Anglia Television
- ☐ Eastern Television
- ☐ STV
- ☐ Thames

3. Which channel began broadcasting in March 1997?
- ☐ BBC3
- ☐ BBC4
- ☐ Channel 4
- ☐ Channel 5

4. Which company took over ATV's Midlands broadcasting?
- ☐ Anglia Television
- ☐ Associated Television
- ☐ Carlton Television
- ☐ Central

5. What did ATV stand for?
- ☐ Allied Television
- ☐ Anglia Television
- ☐ Apalling Television
- ☐ Associated Television

6. On which Radio station is "The Archers" broadcast?

☐ BBC Radio 1
☐ BBC Radio 2
☐ BBC Radio 3
☐ BBC Radio 4

7. What is the Daily Mail's sister Sunday paper called?

☐ Mail on Sunday
☐ News of the World
☐ Observer
☐ Sunday Mail

8. What does BBC stand for?

☐ Big Broadcasting Corporation
☐ British Boat Corporation
☐ British Broadcasting Company
☐ British Broadcasting Corporation

9. In which decade did the BBC begin a TV broadcasting service?

☐ 1920s
☐ 1930s
☐ 1940s
☐ 1950s

10. Which channel was the third UK terrestrial channel?

☐ BBC2
☐ BBC4
☐ Channel 4
☐ ITV

ANSWERS

1 The Sun. 2 Anglia Television. 3 Channel 5. 4 Central. 5 Associated Television. 6 Radio 4. 7 The Mail on Sunday. 8 British Broadcasting Corporation. 9 1930s. 10 BBC 2.

55

Quiz 25: Pop albums

1. Who recorded "Rubber Soul"?
- [ ] The Beatles
- [ ] Bread
- [ ] Iron Maiden
- [ ] The Rolling Stones

2. What goes after "What's the Story" in the title of Oasis's album?
- [ ] Chuck
- [ ] Jackanory
- [ ] Morning Glory
- [ ] Tobermory

3. Which Phil recorded "No Jacket Required"?
- [ ] Collins
- [ ] Daniels
- [ ] Lynott
- [ ] Smith

4. Who recorded "Dark Side of the Moon"?
- [ ] The Beatles
- [ ] Fleetwood Mac
- [ ] Pink Floyd
- [ ] U2

5. Which Rod had six consecutive No. 1 albums in the 70s?
- [ ] Caerphilly
- [ ] Liddle
- [ ] Rogers
- [ ] Stewart

6. Which group had a Night at the Opera and a Day at the Races?

- ☐ Iron Maiden
- ☐ Marx Brothers
- ☐ Queen
- ☐ Squeeze

7. Paul McCartney was in which group for "Band on the Run"?

- ☐ The Beatles
- ☐ Paul's Gang
- ☐ The Quarrymen
- ☐ Wings

8. Who called their greatest hits album "End of Part One"?

- ☐ Kingmaker
- ☐ Oasis
- ☐ Queen
- ☐ Wet Wet Wet

9. Which legendary guitarist recorded "From the Cradle"?

- ☐ Jeff Beck
- ☐ Eric Clapton
- ☐ Jimi Hendrix
- ☐ Jimmy Page

10. Mike Oldfield presented what type of Bells?

- ☐ Hell's
- ☐ Orange
- ☐ Rectangular
- ☐ Tubular

QUIZ 26: KIDS TV

1. Which series dealt with International Rescue and their super aircraft?

☐ Joe 90

☐ The Man From Uncle

☐ Space 1999

☐ Thundebirds

2. Which continent did Paddington Bear come from?

☐ Africa

☐ Europe

☐ North America

☐ South America

3. What sort of animals were Pinky and Perky?

☐ Cats

☐ Dogs

☐ Flowerpot men

☐ Pigs

4. Which programme began "Here is a house. Here is a door. Windows: one, two, three, four"?

☐ Jackanory

☐ Playschool

☐ Rainbow

☐ Vision On

5. What was the number plate on Postman Pat's van?

☐ PAT1

☐ PATTY

☐ PP1

☐ POSTIE1

6. Which show featured Zippy, George plus Rod, Jane & Freddy?

- [ ] Blue Peter
- [ ] Crackerjack
- [ ] Rainbow
- [ ] Sunshine

7. Which show features the tallest, the fastest, the biggest of everything?

- [ ] Crackerjack
- [ ] Magpie
- [ ] Record Breakers
- [ ] Runaround

8. Which Gerry and Sylvia pioneered supermarionation?

- [ ] Anderton
- [ ] Anderson
- [ ] Henson
- [ ] Plath

9. Miss Hoolie, PC Plum and Josie Jump feature on which programme?

- [ ] Bagpuss
- [ ] Balamory
- [ ] Bod
- [ ] Camberwick Green

10. Which podgy cartoon Captain's ship was the Black Pig?

- [ ] Cut-throat Jake
- [ ] Pugwash
- [ ] Sinbad
- [ ] Jack Sparrow

1 "Thunderbirds", 2 (South) America, 3 Piglets, 4 "Playschool", 5 PAT 1, 6 "Rainbow", 7 "Record Breakers", 8 Anderson, 9 "Balamory", 10 Pugwash.

QUIZ 28: POT LUCK

1. Kelvedon Wonder and Little Marvel are types of what?

- [ ] Cabbage
- [ ] Carrot
- [ ] Pea
- [ ] Potato

2. Which programme presented prizes on a conveyor belt?

- [ ] 3–2–1
- [ ] Family Fortunes
- [ ] The Generation Game
- [ ] Keep It In The Family

3. In the 90s, who had a No. 1 with "I Believe"?

- [ ] Hoddle and Waddle
- [ ] Donny Osmond
- [ ] Cliff Richard
- [ ] Robson and Jerome

4. Which veteran comic Eric featured in the Harry Potter films?

- [ ] Chapman
- [ ] Hall
- [ ] Idle
- [ ] Sykes

5. On a Monopoly board, what colour is Pentonville Road?

- [ ] Dark blue
- [ ] Green
- [ ] Light blue
- [ ] Red

6. Who wrote the novel "The Inimitable Jeeves"?

☐ The Reverend W. Awdry
☐ D. H. Lawrence
☐ Evelyn Waugh
☐ P. G. Wodehouse

7. Which of Queen Elizabeth II's children was first to marry?

☐ Andrew
☐ Anne
☐ Charles
☐ Edward

8. What is the administrative centre for the county of Suffolk?

☐ Bury-St-Edmunds
☐ Ipswich
☐ Norwich
☐ Woodbridge

9. In which decade of the 20th century was Joanna Lumley born?

☐ 1920s
☐ 1930s
☐ 1940s
☐ 1950s

10. The sitcom "Yes, Minister" is set in which house?

☐ Bleak House
☐ House of Commons
☐ House of Lords
☐ House of Usher

ANSWERS

1 Pea. 2 "Generation Game". 3 Robson and Jerome. 4 Eric Sykes. 5 Light blue.
6 P. G. Wodehouse. 7 Princess Anne. 8 Ipswich. 9 40s. House of Commons.

61

QUIZ 29: HARRY POTTER

1. The first book title was Harry Potter and what?
- ☐ The Chamber of Secrets
- ☐ The Goblet of Fire
- ☐ The Goblin King
- ☐ The Philosopher's Stone

2. What do J. K. Rowling's initials stand for?
- ☐ Jane Kathleen
- ☐ Joanne Kathleen
- ☐ Joanne Katy
- ☐ Jerome Klapka

3. What is the most popular sport among wizards?
- ☐ Backitch
- ☐ Football
- ☐ Netball
- ☐ Quidditch

4. Which Harry Potter novel was first published in 2005?
- ☐ Harry Potter and the Chamber of Secrets
- ☐ Harry Potter and the Goblet of Fire
- ☐ Harry Potter and the Half Blood Prince
- ☐ Harry Potter and the Prisoner of Azkaban

5. What is the first name of the giant Hagrid?
- ☐ Ragrid
- ☐ Rebus
- ☐ Ruben
- ☐ Rubeus

9 The Sorcerer's Stone, 10 Lord Voldemort

6. Which Emma played Hermione in the Harry Potter films?

☐ Grint
☐ Radcliffe
☐ Simpson
☐ Watson

7. What is Ron's surname?

☐ Granger
☐ Measley
☐ Potter
☐ Weasley

8. What is the third word of all the book titles?

☐ And
☐ In
☐ Of
☐ Potter

9. In the US version what did "The Philosopher's Stone" become in the book title?

☐ The Clever Man
☐ The Philosopher's Book
☐ The Philosopher's Wife
☐ The Sorcerer's Stone

10. Who is "You know who" and "He Who Must not be Named"?

☐ Regulus Black
☐ Hagrid
☐ Harry
☐ Voldemort

QUIZ 30: FOOTBALL

1. What team is known as The Baggies?
- [ ] Bagshot Town
- [ ] Chelsea
- [ ] Liverpool
- [ ] West Bromwich Albion

2. In which year did Arsène Wenger join Arsenal as manager?
- [ ] 1998
- [ ] 1997
- [ ] 1995
- [ ] 1996

3. What two colours are in Derby's home strip?
- [ ] Black and blue
- [ ] Black and green
- [ ] Black and red
- [ ] Black and white

4. Who said, "When seagulls follow the trawler it is because they think the sardines will be thrown into the sea"?
- [ ] Eric Cantona
- [ ] Alex Ferguson
- [ ] Ian Holloway
- [ ] Harry Redknapp

5. Which city has a team of the same name and a United team?
- [ ] Dundee
- [ ] Leicester
- [ ] Manchester
- [ ] Newcastle

6. Hernan Crespo joined Chelsea in 2003 from which club?

☐ AC Milan
☐ Genoa
☐ Inter Milan
☐ Parma

7. Bobby Gould and Phil Neal have both managed which club?

☐ Arsenal
☐ Coventry
☐ Liverpool
☐ Watford

8. Who plays home games at the New Den?

☐ Chelsea
☐ Dennington United
☐ Milwall
☐ West Ham

9. Which club is linked with the playing career of Tom Finney?

☐ Accrington Stanley
☐ Liverpool
☐ Manchester United
☐ Preston North End

10. Who managed Liverpool to the 1986 FA Cup and League double?

☐ Kenny Dalglish
☐ Bob Paisley
☐ Ian Rush
☐ Bill Shankly

ANSWERS

1 West Bromwich Albion. 2 1996. 3 Black and white. 4 Eric Cantona. 5 Dundee.
6 Inter Milan. 7 Coventry. 8 Millwall. 9 Preston. 10 Kenny Dalglish.

QUIZ 31: POLITICS

1. How many years is a Member of Parliament elected for?
- ☐ 2
- ☐ 3
- ☐ 4
- ☐ 5

2. In which year in the 1970s were there two general elections?
- ☐ 1972
- ☐ 1973
- ☐ 1974
- ☐ 1975

3. Which party won Bethnal Green & Bow at the 2005 gen election?
- ☐ Labour
- ☐ New Labour
- ☐ Respect
- ☐ UKIP

4. After the 2005 election had the Liberals got more or fewer parliamentary seats than before?
- ☐ Fewer
- ☐ More
- ☐ None
- ☐ The same

5. Which candidate stood down from the Lib Dem leadership election in 2006?
- ☐ Nick Clegg
- ☐ Chris Huhne
- ☐ Charles Kennedy
- ☐ Mark Oaten

6. Who was Britain's first black woman MP?
☐ Diane Abbott
☐ Rushanara Ali
☐ Dawn Butler
☐ Oona King

7. Who was Tory leader at the time of the 2005 general election?
☐ David Cameron
☐ Michael Howard
☐ John Major
☐ Margaret Thatcher

8. Who became Labour leader after the 1992 election defeat?
☐ Margaret Beckett
☐ Bryan Gould
☐ John Prescott
☐ John Smith

9. Which future PM failed to win Dartford for the Tories in 1950 and 1951?
☐ Tony Benn
☐ Tony Blair
☐ John Major
☐ Margaret Thatcher

10. Which two Davids headed the Alliance party in 1983?
☐ Owen and Jarvis
☐ Owen and Laws
☐ Owen and Steel
☐ Sapphire and Steel

ANSWERS

1 Five years. 2 1974. 3 Respect – The Unity Coalition. 4 More. 5 Mark Oaten. 6 Diane Abbott. 7 Michael Howard. 8 John Smith. 9 Margaret Roberts (Thatcher). 10 Owen, Steel.

67

QUIZ 27: TV TIMES

1. Who was the first permanent female presenter of "Points of View"?

- [ ] Anne Rantzen
- [ ] Esther Rantzen
- [ ] Anne Robinson
- [ ] Terry Wogan

2. Which Team were archaeologists?

- [ ] Archaeology
- [ ] Digging
- [ ] Dream
- [ ] Time

3. Which Ainsley replaced Fern Britton on "Ready Steady Cook"?

- [ ] Barnes
- [ ] Harriott
- [ ] Hayes
- [ ] Smith

4. Which quiz features a picture board and "what happens next"?

- [ ] A League of Their Own
- [ ] A Question of Sport
- [ ] The News Quiz
- [ ] They Think It's All Over

5. Which political programme is based on radio's "Any Questions"?

- [ ] Any Questions
- [ ] Blind Date
- [ ] Points of View
- [ ] Question Time

6. Which Michael presents an eponymous chat show?

☐ Barrymore
☐ Douglas
☐ Hobbs
☐ Parkinson

7. What were the "Spitting Image" puppets made from?

☐ Clay
☐ Paper
☐ Rubber
☐ Wood

8. Which Jennifer partners Dawn French?

☐ Anniston
☐ Beale
☐ Jackson
☐ Saunders

9. Which decade was the setting for "Tenko"?

☐ 1930s
☐ 1940s
☐ 1950s
☐ 1960s

10. Who was the main female presenter of "That's Life"?

☐ Joanna Munro
☐ Esther Rantzen
☐ Anne Robinson
☐ Mollie Sugden

ANSWERS

1 Anne Robinson. 2 Time Team. 3 Harriott. 4 "A Question of Sport". 5 "Question Time". 6 Parkinson. 7 Rubber. 8 Saunders. 9 1940s. 10 Esther Rantzen.

69

Quiz 32: Metal Music

1. Which group was Jimmy Page in before forming Led Zeppelin?

☐ Cream
☐ Hummingbirds
☐ Page and Plant
☐ Yardbirds

2. What was Deep Purple's first hit in the singles charts?

☐ Black Night
☐ Hush
☐ Paranoid
☐ Smoke On The Water

3. What is Ozzy Ozbourne's actual first name?

☐ Dave
☐ John
☐ Ozzy
☐ Ozrick

4. Which group were "Paranoid" in the charts?

☐ Black Sabbath
☐ Coverdale and Page
☐ The Paranoids
☐ Rush

5. Which group took its name from a medieval instrument of torture?

☐ Hammerhead
☐ Iron Maiden
☐ Spinal Tap
☐ Thumbscrew

6. They were known for imaginative cover designs, but what was the title of Led Zeppelin's third album?

☐ Coda
☐ In Through The Out Door
☐ Led Zeppelin II
☐ Led Zeppelin III

7. What nationality is AC/DC singer Brian Johnson?

☐ Australian
☐ English
☐ New Zelander
☐ Scottish

8. Which group founded the Bludgeon Riffola label?

☐ The Bludgeons
☐ Def Leppard
☐ Iron Maiden
☐ Leighton Buzzards

9. Which city did Black Sabbath come from?

☐ Birmingham
☐ Liverpool
☐ London
☐ Manchester

10. Ian Gillan, Graham Bonnet and David Coverdale sang for which group?

☐ Black Sabbath
☐ Coverdale and Page
☐ Deep Purple
☐ Gillan

ANSWERS

1 Yardbirds. 2 Black Night. 3 John. 4 Black Sabbath. 5 Iron Maiden. 6 Led Zeppelin III. 7 Brisih. 8 Def Leppard. 9 Birmingham. 10 Deep Purple.

71

QUIZ 33: ENGLAND

1. Which county did Huntingdonshire become part of in 1974?
- [ ] Buckinhamshire
- [ ] Cambridgeshire
- [ ] Huntingdon
- [ ] Lancashire

2. What is High Wycombe famous for manufacturing?
- [ ] Candles
- [ ] Cars
- [ ] Furniture
- [ ] Shoes

3. Which atomic energy establishment used to be called Windscale?
- [ ] Bradwell
- [ ] Dungeness
- [ ] Sellafield
- [ ] Sizewell

4. In which London borough is Tottenham?
- [ ] Enfield
- [ ] Hackney
- [ ] Haringey
- [ ] Tottenham

5. Which seaside resort is on the Fylde?
- [ ] Blackpool
- [ ] Bridlington
- [ ] Broadchurch
- [ ] Clacton

6. What is the low-lying area of East Anglia called?
- ☐ The Fens
- ☐ The Flats
- ☐ The Lowlands
- ☐ The Wirral

7. Which city was a Roman fortress called Deva and retains its medieval walls?
- ☐ Bath
- ☐ Chester
- ☐ Colchester
- ☐ London

8. How many tunnels under the Mersey link Liverpool to the Wirral?
- ☐ 1
- ☐ 2
- ☐ 3
- ☐ 4

9. In which northern city is the National Railway Museum?
- ☐ Edinburgh
- ☐ Halifax
- ☐ Manchester
- ☐ York

10. The Ribble is the chief river of which county?
- ☐ Cheshire
- ☐ Greater Manchester
- ☐ Lancashire
- ☐ North Yorkshire

ANSWERS

1 Cambridgeshire. 2 Furniture. 3 Sellafield. 4 Haringey. 5 Blackpool. 6 The Fens. 7 Chester. 8 Two. 9 York. 10 Lancashire.

73

QUIZ 34: POT LUCK

1. Which club became the first to win the FA Cup ten times?
☐ Arsenal
☐ Leeds United
☐ Liverpool
☐ Manchester United

2. St Stephen's Day is better known as which day?
☐ Boxing
☐ Christmas
☐ Easter
☐ Steve's

3. Who recorded the original of "Love is All Around"?
☐ Elton John
☐ Elvis Presley
☐ The Troggs
☐ Wet Wet Wet

4. Who became the first First Minister of the new Scottish Parliament?
☐ Keith Brown
☐ Donald Dewar
☐ Fergus Ewing
☐ Alex Salmond

5. A scallop sculpture on Aldeburgh beach in Suffolk is a tribute to which composer?
☐ Benjamin Britten
☐ William Gilbert
☐ Peter Pears
☐ Stephen Sondheim

6. Which Derbyshire town is noted for a church with a crooked spire?

- ☐ Bolsover
- ☐ Buxton
- ☐ Chesterfield
- ☐ Pisa

7. In which field of writing is Simon Armitage mainly concerned?

- ☐ Crime fiction
- ☐ Historical fiction
- ☐ Poetry
- ☐ Science fiction

8. Which sport has its headquarters in St John's Wood, London?

- ☐ Abbey Kempo
- ☐ Cricket
- ☐ Football
- ☐ Tennis

9.The Lutine bell is in which London institution?

- ☐ Harrods
- ☐ House of Commons
- ☐ Kilburn Job Centre
- ☐ Lloyds

10. The inspiration for which children's book character died in April 1996?

- ☐ Winnie the Pooh
- ☐ Harry Potter
- ☐ Christopher Robin
- ☐ Mrs Tiggywinkle

ANSWERS

1 Man Utd. 2 Boxing Day. 3 The Troggs. 4 Donald Dewar. 5 Benjamin Britten. 6 Chesterfield. 7 Poetry. 8 Cricket. 9 Lloyds. 10 Christopher Robin.

NORTHERN

1. In which county is the Giant's Causeway?
- [ ] Antrim
- [ ] Armagh
- [ ] Down
- [ ] Fermanagh

2. What was the shipyard in which the *Titanic* was built?
- [ ] England & Wilf
- [ ] Harland & Wolff
- [ ] Haaaland & Wild
- [ ] Northern Ireland Shipyard Inc.

3. What was the name of the ship built at the same time as the *Titanic*?
- [ ] Classic
- [ ] Jurassic
- [ ] Megalithic
- [ ] Olympic

4. What is Belfast's city airport called?
- [ ] George Best Belfast City Airport
- [ ] Alex Higgins Belfast City Airport
- [ ] Gary Moore Belfast City Airport
- [ ] Van Morrison Belfast City Airport

5. Where was Liam Neeson born?
- [ ] Ballykissangel
- [ ] Ballymena
- [ ] Ballymoney
- [ ] Carrickfergus

IRELAND

6. What is the highest mountain in Northern Ireland?
- [ ] Slieve Bearnagh
- [ ] Slieve Binnian
- [ ] Slieve Commedagh
- [ ] Slieve Donard

7. Which of the following is furthest north?
- [ ] Bangor
- [ ] Ballymena
- [ ] Coleraine
- [ ] Strabane

8. To withing 5 square miles, what is the area of Lough Neagh?
- [ ] 101
- [ ] 111
- [ ] 151
- [ ] 176

9. Which of the following is *not* in Northern Ireland?
- [ ] Ballybeg Castle
- [ ] Ballygally Castle
- [ ] Gosford Castle
- [ ] Killymoon Castle

10. Who is the patron saint of Northern Ireland?
- [ ] St Andrew
- [ ] St George
- [ ] St Edward
- [ ] St Patrick

ANSWERS

1 Antrim. 2 Harland & Wolff. 3 Olympic. 4 George Best Belfast City Airport. 5 Ballymena. 6 Slieve Donard. 7 Coleraine. 8 151. 9 Ballybeg. 10 St Patrick.

77

QUIZ 36: TV COPPERS

1. In which city is "Taggart" set?
☐ Dundee
☐ Edinburgh
☐ Glasgow
☐ New York

2. What is "The Bill"'s DI Burnside's first name?
☐ Bernard
☐ Dave
☐ Frank
☐ Tosh

3. Who was co-creator of "Hazell" with Gordon Williams?
☐ Nicholas Ball
☐ Charles Dickens
☐ Harry Redknapp
☐ Terry Venables

4. Which police series had the theme music "An Ordinary Copper"?
☐ Dickson of Dock Green
☐ Thieftakers
☐ The Wire
☐ Z Cars

5. Who created the character of Chief Inspector Wexford?
☐ Agatha Christie
☐ G. K. Chesterton
☐ Ruth Newman
☐ Ruth Rendell

6. Which actor links "The Chief" and "The Professionals"?
- [ ] Lewis Collins
- [ ] Gordon Jackson
- [ ] Martin Shaw
- [ ] Christopher Timothy

7. What was Bergerac's first name?
- [ ] Jim
- [ ] Jonathan
- [ ] Piers
- [ ] Roland

8. Who played the part of Jericho in the 2005 series?
- [ ] Robbie Coltrane
- [ ] James Jericho
- [ ] Robert Lindsay
- [ ] Lindsay Roberts

9. Whom did Spender work for before being posted back to Newcastle?
- [ ] Metropolitan Police
- [ ] MI5
- [ ] MI6
- [ ] The Sweeney

10. In which series did Jean Darblay, then Kate Longton, appear?
- [ ] The Bill
- [ ] Jenny Bravo
- [ ] Juliet Bravo
- [ ] The Thin Blue Line

1 Glasgow. 2 Frank. 3 Terry Venables. 4 Dixon of Dock Green. 5 Ruth Rendell. 6. Martin Shaw. 7 Jim. 8 Robert Lindsay. 9 Metropolitan Police. 10 Juliet Bravo.

QUIZ 37: KIDS TV

1. What is the longest-running children's TV programme?

☐ Blue Peter
☐ Newsround
☐ The Simpsons
☐ Tomorrow's World

2. Who host Dick and Dom in "Da Bungalow"?

☐ Frank McCourt and Dominic Hyde
☐ Richard McCourt & Dominic Wood
☐ Dick Turpin and Dom Perignon
☐ Richard Wood & Dominic McCourt

3. "Can We Fix It" relates to which handyman?

☐ Bill
☐ Bob
☐ Jim
☐ Vlad

4. In which country is "Balamory" set?

☐ England
☐ Northern Ireland
☐ Scotland
☐ Wales

5. Which village's postmistress is called Mrs Goggins?

☐ Camberwick Green
☐ Greendale
☐ Greenvale
☐ Tobermory

6. What was "Fingermouse" made from?

- ☐ Bricks
- ☐ Clay
- ☐ Cloth
- ☐ Paper

7. Who fought against Bulk and Texas Pete?

- ☐ Buzz Lightyear
- ☐ Dangermouse
- ☐ Metal Mickey
- ☐ SuperTed

8. Who presented his own "Cartoon Time" and "Cartoon Club"?

- ☐ John Craven
- ☐ Rolf Harris
- ☐ Tony Hart
- ☐ Morph

9. Which of these is NOT a singer from "Rainbow"?

- ☐ Freddy
- ☐ Jane
- ☐ Rod
- ☐ Zippy

10. Which show famously ended with "Bye bye, everybody, bye bye"?

- ☐ Animal Hospital
- ☐ Crackerjack
- ☐ The Rod Hull and Emu Show
- ☐ Sooty

ANSWERS

1 Blue Peter. 2 Richard McCourt & Dominic Wood. 3 Bob the Builder. 4 Scotland. 5 Greendale. 6 Paper. 7 SuperTed. 8 Rolf Harris. 9 Rod, Jane and Freddy. 10 Sooty.

81

QUIZ 38: WAR

1. In which month in 1914 did the First World War begin?
- [ ] July
- [ ] August
- [ ] September
- [ ] October

2. What were people told to "keep burning" in the 1914 song?
- [ ] Books
- [ ] Germans
- [ ] Home fires
- [ ] Wood

3. What was the occupation of Edith Cavell, who was shot by the Germans on a spying charge?
- [ ] Comfort woman
- [ ] Doctor
- [ ] Nurse
- [ ] Writer

4. Who became Prime Minister of Britain in 1916?
- [ ] Lloyd George
- [ ] Harold Lloyd
- [ ] Ramsay MacDonald
- [ ] Harold MacMillan

5. What did George V ban in his household to encourage others to do the same, and help the war effort?
- [ ] Alcohol
- [ ] Beans
- [ ] Fire
- [ ] Petrol

6. In the 1915 song where did you "Pack Up Your Troubles"?
- [ ] In your face
- [ ] In your old dirt bag
- [ ] In your old kit bag
- [ ] In the Kaiser's bum

7. How did Lord Kitchener die?
- [ ] Blown up
- [ ] Lost at sea
- [ ] Poisoned
- [ ] Shot by sniper

8. At which battle in 1916 were there said to be a million fatalities?
- [ ] Arras
- [ ] Gallipoli
- [ ] Jutland
- [ ] The Somme

9. Which new weapon was introduced in battle in 1916?
- [ ] Flame thrower
- [ ] Machine gun
- [ ] Mortar
- [ ] Tank

10. What was the 1914–18 war known as until 1939?
- [ ] The Best War Ever
- [ ] The Grand War
- [ ] The Great War
- [ ] The Superb War

ANSWERS

1 August. 2 Home fires. 3 Nurse. 4 Lloyd George. 5 Alcohol. 6 In your old kit bag. 7 Lost at sea. 8 Somme. 9 Tank. 10 The Great War.

QUIZ 39: CRICKET

1. What does the first C stand for in TCCB?
- [ ] Charles
- [ ] Classic
- [ ] Cheshire
- [ ] County

2. In which year did Michael Vaughan take over as England captain?
- [ ] 2000
- [ ] 2001
- [ ] 2002
- [ ] 2003

3. Who was the last cricketer to be named BBC Sports Personality of the Year before Freddie Flintoff?
- [ ] Ian Botham
- [ ] Freddie Flintoff
- [ ] Graham Gooch
- [ ] W. G. Grace

4. Which lady sang on the 2005 England version of "Jerusalem"?
- [ ] Adele
- [ ] Keedie
- [ ] Kylie
- [ ] Katy Perry

5. Which popular figure wrote "My Spin on Cricket"?
- [ ] Jonathan Agnew
- [ ] Richie Benaud
- [ ] Geoff Boycott
- [ ] Monty Panesar

6. What was remarkable about the 16 overs that South Africa's Hugh Tayfield bowled against England at Durban in 1957?

☐ Every ball was hit for 4
☐ Every ball was hit for 6
☐ All maidens
☐ All wides

7. Who was England's youngest and oldest post-war Test player?

☐ Brian Close
☐ Freddie Laker
☐ Jim Laker
☐ Brian Statham

8. Who skippered Pakistan in the 2005 victory over England?

☐ Kamran Akmal
☐ Inzamam ul-Haq
☐ Younis Khan
☐ Abdul Razzaq

9. In 1995, Jack Russell took how many catches in a Test to create a new world record?

☐ 9
☐ 10
☐ 11
☐ 12

10. Which county did Ian Botham NOT play for?

☐ Durham
☐ Essex
☐ Somerset
☐ Worcestershire

QUIZ 40: SCOTLAND

1. Edradour is the smallest what in Scotland?
- ☐ Distillery
- ☐ Mountain
- ☐ Person
- ☐ River

2. Which famous Scottish writer lived at Abbotsford by the Tweed?
- ☐ Robert Burns
- ☐ Walter Kennedy
- ☐ Sir Walter Scott
- ☐ Irving Welsh

3. In which direction from Edinburgh do the Pentland Hills lie?
- ☐ Northwest
- ☐ Northeast
- ☐ Southwest
- ☐ Southeast

4. What is Berwick Law?
- ☐ Arcane legislation
- ☐ Extinct volcano
- ☐ A legal company
- ☐ A person

5. What is the Bass Rock famous as?
- ☐ Bird sanctuary
- ☐ Brewery
- ☐ Distillery
- ☐ Zoo

6. Which cathedral is also known as the High Kirk of Edinburgh?

☐ St Andrew
☐ St Giles
☐ St John
☐ St Patrick

7. Rothesay is the chief town of which island?

☐ Arran
☐ Bute
☐ Cara
☐ Davaar

8. What is at the foot of the Royal Mile in Edinburgh?

☐ Edinburgh Castle
☐ Holyrood House
☐ Hollywood House
☐ Holyrood Island

9. Which city is at the mouth of the rivers Don and Dee?

☐ Aberdeen
☐ Dumfries
☐ Edinburgh
☐ Glasgow

10. What is produced at Torness?

☐ Beer
☐ Kilts
☐ Nuclear Power
☐ Whisky

ANSWERS

1 Distillery. 2 Sir Walter Scott. 3 Southwest. 4 Extinct volcano. 5 Bird sanctuary.
6 St Giles Cathedral. 7 Bute. 8 Holyrood House. 9 Aberdeen. 10 Nuclear power.

87

QUIZ 41: TV COMEDY

1. Which Ashley was named best Comedy Actress in the 2005 British Comedy Awards?
☐ Ashley Benson
☐ Ashley Jensen
☐ Ashley Madekwe
☐ Ashley Spalding

2. Who created the series "Extras" with Ricky Gervais?
☐ David Bowie
☐ Stephen Merchant
☐ Karl Pilkington
☐ Paul Whitehouse

3. Which show had the spoof "Five Go Mad in Dorset"?
☐ The Comic Strip Presents
☐ The Enid Blyton Show
☐ Tales of the Unexpected
☐ The Twilight Zone

4. Name the first two regular team captains in "Have I Got News for You?"?
☐ Paul Merton & Ian Duncan Smith
☐ Paul Merton & Ian Hislop
☐ Paul Merton & Ian Paisley
☐ Paul Simon & Art Garfunkel

5. Who created Algernon the Rasta and the Reverend Nat West?
☐ Jim Davidson
☐ Dawn French
☐ Lenny Henry
☐ Paul Whitehouse

6. Which writer hosts the ITV predecessor of "Auntie's Bloomers"?

☐ Dave Allen
☐ Harry Hill
☐ Denis Norden
☐ Nicholas Parsons

7. Who created Lauren, the schoolgirl from hell?

☐ Dawn French
☐ Jennifer Saunders
☐ Pamela Stephenson
☐ Catherine Tate

8. What was Peter Cook and Dudley Moore's revue show called?

☐ Derek and Clive Live
☐ Not Only ... But Also
☐ That Was The Week That Was
☐ The Two Peters

9. What is the surname of the family in "My Family"?

☐ Harper
☐ Jones
☐ Sharper
☐ Smith

10. Who was the resident vocalist on "That Was the Week That was"?

☐ David Frost
☐ Roy Kinnear
☐ Millicent Martin
☐ Richard Stillgoe

ANSWERS

1 Ashley Jensen. 2 Stephen Merchant. 3 The Comic Strip Presents. 4 Paul Merton, Ian Hislop. 5 Lenny Henry. 6 Denis Norden. 7 Catherine Tate. 8 Not Only ... But Also.

89

Quiz 42: Pop Music

1. Who was lead singer with Style Council?
- [ ] Dee C. Lee
- [ ] Mick Talbot
- [ ] Paul Weller
- [ ] Steve White

2. Who sang with Dave Dee, Beaky, Mick and Tich?
- [ ] Doc
- [ ] Dozy
- [ ] Droopy
- [ ] Dreamy

3. Who brought out the album "A Present for Everyone" in 2003?
- [ ] Blue
- [ ] Busted
- [ ] East 17
- [ ] JLS

4. What was the first top ten hit single for The Darkness?
- [ ] Dream On
- [ ] Get Your Hands Off My Woman
- [ ] I Believe In A Thing Called Love
- [ ] Love Is Only A Feeling

5. Which group featured Dave Gilmour and Roger Waters?
- [ ] Led Zeppelin
- [ ] Pink Floyd
- [ ] Rush
- [ ] The Wall

6. What was Take That's first No 1?

☐ Light My Fire
☐ Pray
☐ Rock DJ
☐ Stay

7. Who was the Who's original drummer?

☐ John Bonham
☐ Keith Moon
☐ Ringo Starr
☐ Pete Townshend

8. Which group formed their own label Dep International?

☐ The Depps
☐ The Beat
☐ Madness
☐ UB40

9. Merrill, Jay, Wayne, Jimmy and Donny made up which group?

☐ The Coors
☐ Fleetwood Mac
☐ Jacksons
☐ Osmonds

10. Which Kinks hit starts, "Dirty old river, must you keep rolling..."?

☐ Lazing On A Sunny Afternoon
☐ Lola
☐ Waterloo Sunset
☐ You Really Got Me

Quiz 43: England

1. What did Sunderland become in 1992 which Manchester, Liverpool and Birmingham became in the 19th century?

☐ Bankrupt
☐ A city
☐ Part of the United Kingdom
☐ A city with a football team in the UK's top division

2. Which river runs through London?

☐ Colne
☐ Ouse
☐ Stour
☐ Thames

3.Which is furthest north, Southport or Northampton?

☐ Eastbourne
☐ High Green
☐ Northampton
☐ Southport

4. Which stretch of water divides England and France?

☐ English Channel
☐ French Channel
☐ Irish Sea
☐ North Sea

5. What do the letters NEC stand for?

☐ National Elephant Centre
☐ National Exhibition Centre
☐ National Exhibition Control
☐ Natural Exhibition Centre

6. What is the area around Stoke-on-Trent known as?

- ☐ Derbyshire
- ☐ The Potteries
- ☐ The Potties
- ☐ Stoke City

7. Which northern city is served by Ringway airport?

- ☐ Liverpool
- ☐ Manchester
- ☐ Newcastle
- ☐ Sunderland

8. Which motorway starts south of Birmingham and goes north-west towards Scotland?

- ☐ M1
- ☐ M16
- ☐ M6
- ☐ M61

9. Which part of the country would a Geordie come from?

- ☐ South
- ☐ West
- ☐ Northeast
- ☐ Southeast

10. Near which large city would you find the Wirral?

- ☐ Bristol
- ☐ Leeds
- ☐ Liverpool
- ☐ Newcastle

ANSWERS

1 A city. 2 Thames. 3 Southport. 4 English Channel. 5 National Exhibition Centre. 6 The Potteries. 7 Manchester. 8 M6. 9 Northeast. 10 Liverpool.

QUIZ 44: NARNIA

1. How many Chronicles of Narnia are there?

- [ ] 4
- [ ] 5
- [ ] 6
- [ ] 7

2. Who voiced Aslan in the 2005 film "The Lion, the Witch and the Wardrobe"?

- [ ] John Cleese
- [ ] Morgan Freeman
- [ ] Jude Law
- [ ] Liam Neeson

3. What is the name of the castle housing the four thrones?

- [ ] Cair Paravel
- [ ] Care Less
- [ ] Four Thrones Keep
- [ ] Hatfield Peverel

4. Digory and Polly appear in which book?

- [ ] Prince Caspian
- [ ] The Lion, the Witch and the Wardrobe
- [ ] The Magician's Nephew
- [ ] Voyage of the Dawn Treader

5. Which season is Narnia in at the start of "The Lion, the Witch and the Wardrobe"?

- [ ] Spring
- [ ] Summer
- [ ] Autumn
- [ ] Winter

6. What sort of animal is Reepicheep?

- ☐ Talking cat
- ☐ Talking chicken
- ☐ Talking lion
- ☐ Talking mouse

7. In the later Chronicles how is Digory better known?

- ☐ Dig
- ☐ Digory Pigory
- ☐ The Professor
- ☐ The Teacher

8. What mode of transport is the Dawn Treader?

- ☐ Airship
- ☐ Car
- ☐ Steamroller
- ☐ Ship

9. What is the real name of the White Witch?

- ☐ Avant
- ☐ Fenris Ulf
- ☐ Jadis
- ☐ Maugrim

10. Who is the eldest of the Pevensie children?

- ☐ Edmund
- ☐ Lucy
- ☐ Peter
- ☐ Susan

—————————————————— ANSWERS

1 Seven. 2 Liam Neeson. 3 Cair Paravel. 4 The Magician's Nephew. 5 Winter. 6 Talking mouse. 7 The Professor. 8 Ship. 9 Jadis. 10 Peter.

95

QUIZ 45: THE UK

1. How many faces has the clock on Big Ben's tower?
- [ ] 1
- [ ] 2
- [ ] 3
- [x] 4

2. In which port were Dickens and Brunel both born?
- [ ] Bristol
- [ ] Bournemouth
- [x] Portsmouth
- [ ] Southampton

3. In which London building is the Lord Mayor's banquet held?
- [ ] 10 Downing Street
- [ ] Buckingham Palace
- [x] Guildhall
- [ ] Royal Festival Hall

4. Which Womble was named after the town on the Isle of Mull?
- [ ] Uncle Bulgaria
- [ ] Madame Cholet
- [ ] Tobermory
- [ ] Tomsk

5. Which Channel Island is famous for having no cars?
- [ ] Alderney
- [ ] Guernesey
- [ ] Jersey
- [x] Sark

6. Where is Beaumaris Castle?

☐ Anglesey
☐ Isle of Man
☐ Isle of Wight
☐ Mull

7. Girton and Newnham are colleges of which university?

☐ Aston
☐ Cambridge
☐ Manchester
☐ Oxford

8. What is the tallest building in London called?

☑ Lloyds Building
☐ The London Eye
☐ The Shard
☐ The Spike

9. Bryher is part of which islands?

☐ Bristol Channel
☐ Farne Islands
☐ Islands of Furness
☐ Scillies

10. Which Hills divide England and Scotland?

☐ The Borders
☑ Cheviots
☐ Munros
☐ Snowdonia

ANSWERS

1 Four. 2 Portsmouth. 3 Guildhall. 4 Tobermory. 5 Sark. 6 Anglesea. 7. Cambridge. 8. Lloyds. 9 Scillies. 10 Cheviots.

97

QUIZ 46: WALES

1. Which creature of legend is seen on the Welsh flag?

☐ Dove
☐ Dragon
☐ Giant
☐ Unicorn

2. Which city in the south of the country is its second largest?

☐ Cardiff
☐ Harlech
☐ Port Talbot
☐ Swansea

3. Which sport is played at Cardiff Arms Park?

☐ Cricket
☐ Cycling
☐ Football
☐ Rugby

4. Which wild cat gives its name to a Bay on Cardiff's quayside?

☐ Lion
☐ Manx
☐ Puma
☐ Tiger

5. The production of which fuel affected the Welsh landscape until its decline in recent years?

☐ Coal
☐ Oil
☐ Peat
☐ Wood

6. Who was invested as Prince of Wales in 1969 at Caernarvon Castle?

☐ Andrew
☐ Charles
☐ Edward
☐ Phillip

7. Which vegetable is a Welsh emblem?

☐ Cabbage
☐ Leek
☐ Pea
☐ Potato

8. Which country lies to the east of Wales?

☐ England
☐ Ireland
☐ Northern Ireland
☐ Scotland

9. Who is the patron saint of Wales?

☐ Andrew
☐ David
☐ James
☐ Patrick

10. What is the mountainous area around Snowdon called?

☐ Snowdonia
☐ Snowdonland
☐ Snowdon Mountains
☐ The Snowies

ANSWERS

1 Dragon. 2 Swansea. 3 Rugby. 4 Tiger. 5 Coal. 6 Prince Charles. 7 Leek. 8 England. 9 St David. 10 Snowdonia.

99

QUIZ 47: FOOTBALL

1. At which Premiership club did Dunn and Duff play in the same side?
- ☑ Blackburn Rovers
- ☐ Chelsea
- ☐ Newcastle United
- ☐ Sunderland

2. David James played in goal for which London club?
- ☐ Chelsea
- ☐ QPR
- ☐ Reading
- ☑ West Ham

3. At which club did Steve Bruce take over from Trevor Francis?
- ☑ Birmingham
- ☐ Ipswich Town
- ☐ Manchester United
- ☐ Sunderland

4. Keeper Chris Woods set a British record for clean sheets at which club?
- ☐ Celtic
- ☑ Rangers
- ☐ Sunderland
- ☐ West Bromwich Albion

5. Who became the first female football club managing director?
- ☑ Karren Brady
- ☐ Rita Brady
- ☐ Millie Jacobson
- ☐ Hope Powell

6. Who was manager when Ipswich first won the FA Cup?
- [ ] Brian Clough
- [ ] Trevor Francis
- [ ] Bobby Moore
- [x] Bobby Robson

7. Stan Collymore won his first England cap while at which club?
- [ ] Aston Villa
- [x] Nottingham Forest
- [ ] Liverpool
- [ ] Real Oviedo

8. Which former Manchester United star also turned out for Fulham and Hibs?
- [ ] David Beckham
- [ ] Dimitar Berbatov
- [x] George Best
- [ ] Cristiano Ronaldo

9. Man Utd legend Peter Schmeichel played for which country?
- [ ] Denmark
- [ ] Estonia
- [ ] Finland
- [ ] Sweden

10. What was Gazza's first London club?
- [ ] Arsenal
- [ ] Chelsea
- [x] Spurs
- [ ] West Ham

ANSWERS

1 Blackburn Rovers. 2 West Ham. 3 Birmingham. 4 Rangers. 5 Karren Brady 6 Bobby Robson. 7 Nottingham Forest. 8 George Best. 9 Denmark. 10 Spurs.

101

QUIZ 48: SCOTLAND

1. What are the Cairngorms?

☐ Hills
☐ Islands
☐ Mountains
☐ Rivers

2. Which east coast port is known as the Granite City?

☐ Aberdeen
☐ Edinburgh
☐ Graniteen
☐ John O'Groats

3. Which islands give their name to ponies and wool?

☐ Arran
☐ Curly
☐ Dartmoor
☐ Shetland

4. In which Loch is there said to be a monster?

☐ Cup
☐ Lomond
☐ Nabar
☐ Ness

5. Which Isle was linked to the mainland by a bridge in 1995?

☐ Arran
☐ Lewis
☐ Mull
☐ Skye

6. Which Mull was the title of a song by Paul McCartney?

- [ ] Mull of Kintyre
- [ ] Isle of Mull
- [ ] Mull of the Dump
- [ ] Sound of Mull

7. Which river flows through Glasgow?

- [ ] Clyde
- [ ] Esk
- [ ] Forth
- [ ] Tay

8. Which city holds an annual Arts Festival?

- [ ] Aberdeen
- [ ] Dundee
- [ ] Edinburgh
- [ ] Glasgow

9. Which speciality's ingredients include sheep's stomach and oatmeal?

- [ ] Haggis
- [ ] Oatcakes
- [ ] Toffee
- [ ] Whisky

10. Which village was a popular destination for runaway couples?

- [ ] Bride
- [ ] Gretna Green
- [ ] Holmfirth
- [ ] Wedding

QUIZ 50: SOAPS

1. In "EastEnders", which Jim married Dot?
☐ Bradley
☐ Branning
☐ Brent
☐ Cotton

2. What is the name of Jack and Vera Duckworth's wayward son?
☐ Arthur
☐ David
☐ Mike
☐ Terry

3. In "Corrie", which double-barrelled name did Les and Cilla have?
☐ Batley-Brown
☐ Battenburg-Brown
☐ Battersby-Brown
☐ Lincoln-Brown

4. Which former Mrs Liam Gallagher appeared in "Emmerdale"?
☐ Nicole Appleton
☐ Samantha Giles
☐ Patsy Kensit
☐ Sadie King

5. Which Battersby sister returned to "Corrie" in 2004?
☐ Cilla
☐ Janice
☐ Leanne
☐ Toyah

6. What is the name of the Barbara Windsor character in "EastEnders"?

- [ ] Glenda Mitchell
- [ ] Louise Mitchell
- [ ] Peggy Mitchell
- [ ] Sam Mitchell

7. Which soap has an underwear factory called Underworld?

- [ ] Coronation Street
- [ ] Eastenders
- [ ] Emmerdale
- [ ] Neighbours

8. Where was Curly's wife Raquel heading for on leaving Weatherfield?

- [ ] Costa del Sol
- [ ] Gretna Green
- [ ] Malaysia
- [ ] Singapore

9. Which C is the setting for "Hollyoaks"?

- [ ] Chesterfield
- [ ] Chelmsford
- [ ] Chester
- [ ] Colchester

10. Which soap pub is famous for its Newton & Ridley beer?

- [ ] The Queen's Head
- [ ] The Queen Victoria
- [ ] The Rovers Return
- [ ] The Woolpack

ANSWERS

1 Branning. 2 Terry. 3 Battersby-Brown. 4 Patsy Kensit. 5 Leanne. 6 Peggy Mitchell. 7 "Coronation Street". 8 Malaysia. 9 Chester. 10 The Rovers Return.

105

QUIZ 51: UK TV

1. Who hosted "Crimewatch UK" with Nick Ross prior to Jill Dando?
- [ ] Fiona Bruce
- [ ] Sue Cook
- [ ] Esther Rantzen
- [ ] Kirsty Young

2. Which "EastEnders" character was played by Ray Brooks?
- [ ] Jack
- [ ] Jill
- [ ] Jim
- [ ] Joe

3. Who is the priest played by Stephen Tomkinson in "Ballykissangel"?
- [ ] Frank MacAnally
- [ ] Aidan O'Connell
- [ ] Peter Clifford
- [ ] Frankie Sullivan

4. What is the name of BBC TV's long-running sports quiz show?
- [ ] A League of their Own
- [ ] A Question of Sport
- [ ] A Question of Sport Time
- [ ] Sport in Question

5. Which Martin played Judge John Deed?
- [ ] Deed
- [ ] Dixon
- [ ] Jarvis
- [ ] Shaw

6. Who left "Blue Peter" to join the "Clothes Show" team?
- [ ] John Noakes
- [ ] Helen Skelton
- [ ] Anthea Turner
- [ ] Tim Vincent

7. Who is known as "Mr Trick Shot"?
- [ ] John Parrott
- [ ] Dennis Taylor
- [ ] Willie Thorne
- [ ] John Virgo

8. Who starred as Blanco in "Porridge"?
- [ ] Christopher Biggins
- [ ] Ronnie Barker
- [ ] David Jason
- [ ] Fulton MacKay

9.Which TV star's first record release was "Extremis"?
- [ ] Gillian Anderson
- [ ] Chris Carter
- [ ] David Duchovny
- [ ] Rosamund Pike

10. Who won "Celebrity Big Brother" at the start of 2006?
- [ ] Faria Alam
- [ ] George Galloway
- [ ] Chantelle Houghton
- [ ] Dennis Rodman

ANSWERS

1 Sue Cook. 2 Joe. 3 Peter Clifford. 4 A Question of Sport. 5 Shaw. 6 Tim Vincent.
7 John Virgo. 8 David Jason. 9 Gillian Anderson. 10 Chantelle Houghton.

107

QUIZ 52: FOOD

1. What type of cheese is Stilton?
- [ ] Blue
- [ ] Green
- [ ] Hard
- [ ] Mouldy

2. What do you add to milk to make porridge?
- [ ] Gruel
- [ ] Oats
- [ ] Sugar
- [ ] Whisky

3. What is minestrone?
- [ ] Cheese
- [ ] Noodles
- [ ] A type of potoato
- [ ] Soup

4. What is bottled tomato sauce called?
- [ ] Brown sauce
- [ ] HP sauce
- [ ] Ketchup
- [ ] Piccalilli

5. What colour is gin?
- [ ] Colourless
- [ ] Blue
- [ ] Green
- [ ] Yellow

6. Which fruit is covered with toffee at a fairground?

☐ Apple
☐ Banana
☐ Carrot
☐ Pear

7. Which nuts are used to make marzipan?

☐ Almonds
☐ Chestnuts
☐ Hazelnuts
☐ Walnuts

8. How is a Spotted Dick usually eaten?

☐ Hot
☐ Cold
☐ With cheese
☐ In a wafer

9. What meat dish is Cumberland famous for?

☐ Bacon
☐ Deep-fried Mars bars
☐ Ribs
☐ Sausage

10. How is most bread sold in supermarkets?

☐ Frozen
☐ Sliced
☐ Stale
☐ Toasted

ANSWERS

1 Blue. 2 Oats. 3 Soup. 4 Ketchup. 5 Colourless. 6 Apples.
7 Almonds. 8 Hot. 9 Sausage. 10 Sliced.

QUIZ 53: ROYALS

1. In which country did Charles and Camilla spend their honeymoon?
- [ ] England
- [ ] Northern Ireland
- [ ] Scotland
- [ ] Wales

2. Who is the first female in line to the throne?
- [ ] Princess Anne
- [ ] Princess Beatrice
- [ ] Princess Eugenie
- [ ] Princess Michael

3. Which King (name and number) was the subject of a 1995 film?
- [ ] George III
- [ ] George IV
- [ ] Edward VII
- [ ] Henry VIII

4. Who are the parents of Lady Helen Taylor?
- [ ] Duke and Duchess of Birmingham
- [ ] Duke and Duchess of Cornwall
- [ ] Duke and Duchess of Kent
- [ ] Duke and Duchess of York

5. Who played John Brown when Judi Dench was Victoria on TV?
- [ ] Billy Connolly
- [ ] Geoffrey Palmer
- [ ] Antony Sher
- [ ] David Westhead

6. Who interviewed Princess Diana for "Panorama" in 1995?

- ☐ Martin Bashir
- ☐ David Frost
- ☐ Michael Parkinson
- ☐ Terry Wogan

7. Princess Diana confessed to having had an affair with whom?

- ☐ Dodi Al Fayed
- ☐ James Gilbey
- ☐ James Hewitt
- ☐ Andrew Morton

8. Who was Princess Anne's bridesmaid when she married Mark Phillips?

- ☐ Lady Sarah Armstrong-Jones
- ☐ Prince Edward
- ☐ Princess Margaret
- ☐ Lady Diana Spencer

9. Who was Serena Linley's mother-in-law?

- ☐ Princess Anne
- ☐ Queen Elizabeth
- ☐ Princess Margaret
- ☐ The Queen Mother

10. How many lots were there in the Christie's sale of Diana's dresses?

- ☐ 5
- ☐ 13
- ☐ 79
- ☐ 101

ANSWERS

1 Scotland. 2 Princess Beatrice. 3 George III. 4 Duke and Duchess of Kent. 5 Billy Connolly. 6 Martin Bashir. 7 James Hewitt. 8 Lady Sarah Armstrong-Jones.

111

QUIZ 54: BOOKS

1. What was the first book in English to be printed in England?
- [ ] The Bible
- [ ] The Canterbury Tales
- [ ] The Complete Works of Shakespeare
- [ ] The Oxford English Dictionary

2. Which books do castaways automatically receive on "Desert Island Discs"?
- [ ] The Bible and the Koran
- [ ] The Bible and the complete works of Shakespeare
- [ ] Mein Kampf and the Bible
- [ ] The Koran and the complete works of Shakespeare

3. Who was responsible for "The Complete Hip and Thigh Diet"?
- [ ] Rosemary Conley
- [ ] Hilary Jones
- [ ] Coleen Nolan
- [ ] Katie Price

4. In which century was the "Oxford English Dictionary" started in earnest?
- [ ] 18th
- [ ] 19th
- [ ] 20th
- [ ] 21st

5. Whose third novel was entitled "Beyond Beauty"?
- [ ] Martin Amis
- [ ] David Foster Wallace
- [ ] Hilary Mantel
- [ ] Zadie Smith

9 Colleen McCullough. 10 Not a Penny More, not a Penny Less.

6. Which British publisher launched Penguin titles in 1935?

☐ André Deutsch
☐ Allen Lane
☐ Penny Lane
☐ Arthur Penguin

7. In which decade did Guinness start to publish their "Book of Records" annually?

☐ 1950s
☐ 1960s
☐ 1970s
☐ 1980s

8. Who began publishing Beatrix Potter's books in 1902?

☐ Enid Blyton
☐ Allen Lane
☐ Penguin
☐ Frederick Warne

9. Who wrote "The Thorn Birds"?

☐ Jeffery Archer
☐ Richard Chamberlain
☐ Colleen McCullough
☐ Rachel Ward

10. What was Jeffrey Archer's first successful novel?

☐ First Among Equals
☐ In and Out of Court
☐ Kane and Abel
☐ Not a Penny More, Not a Penny Less

ANSWERS

1 The Canterbury Tales. 2 The Bible and the complete works of Shakespeare. 3 Rosemary Conley. 4 19th. 5 Zadie Smith. 6 Allen Lane. 7 1960s. 8 Frederick Warne.

113

1. Who first played the title role in "Evita" in the West End?

☐ Barbara Dixon

☐ Jason Donovan

☐ Elaine Paige

☐ Mandy Patinkin

2. In which musical does Fagin appear?

☐ Les Misérables

☐ Miss Saigon

☐ Oliver!

☐ The Phantom of the Opera

3. Which Arthur wrote "Death of a Salesman", a play revived in the West End in 2005?

☐ Cooper

☐ Daley

☐ Miller

☐ Williams

4. he Importance of Being '?' is the name of an Oscar Wilde play?

☐ Earnest

☐ Ernest

☐ Erstwhile

☐ Gay

5. Which girl is the lecturer Educating in the play by Willy Russell?

☐ Jane

☐ Rita

☐ Sue

☐ Sunita

THEATRE

6. What is the full name of the show often just referred to as Les Mis?

- [ ] Le Misanthrope
- [ ] Les Misérables
- [ ] Les Mistakes
- [ ] The Saddoes

7. Aspects of what are the theme of which Lloyd Webber musical?

- [ ] Cats
- [ ] Grime
- [ ] Hate
- [ ] Love

8. What meat appears in a Punch & Judy show?

- [ ] Bacon
- [ ] Crocodile steak
- [ ] Pork chop
- [ ] Sausages

9. Who composed 'Peter Grimes'?

- [ ] Benjamin Britten
- [ ] Peter Pears
- [ ] Andrew Lloyd Webber
- [ ] Julian Lloyd Webber

10. Who does the Beast fall in love with?

- [ ] A mirror
- [ ] Beauty
- [ ] Himself
- [ ] Ugly

ANSWERS

9 Benjamin Britten. 10 Beauty.

1 Elaine Paige. 2 Oliver! 3 Miller. 4 Earnest. 5 Rita. 6 Les Misérables. 7 Love. 8 Sausages.

115

QUIZ 49: CRICKET

1. How many bails are there on a set of wickets?
- [ ] 1
- [ ] 2
- [ ] 3
- [ ] 4

2. Which county does Geoff Boycott come from?
- [ ] Devon
- [ ] Essex
- [ ] Suffolk
- [ ] Yorkshire

3. Trent Bridge is in which English city?
- [ ] Liverpool
- [ ] London
- [ ] Manchester
- [ ] Nottingham

4. How many runs are scored in a maiden over?
- [ ] 0
- [ ] 1
- [ ] 2
- [ ] 3

5. What were the initials of legendary Victorian cricketer Dr Grace?
- [ ] D. W.
- [ ] W. C.
- [ ] W. G.
- [ ] W. I.

6. Which county did Michael Vaughan play for?

☐ Cambridgeshire
☐ Essex
☐ Northamptonshire
☐ Yorkshire

7. In the 1990s, which Alec has opened and kept wicket for England?

☐ Baldwin
☐ Guinness
☐ Jones
☐ Stewart

8. In scoring, what does c & b stand for?

☐ Catch and bowl
☐ Campbell and Browne
☐ Caught and bowled
☐ Classic and bright

9. Which English county did West Indies skipper Clive Lloyd play for?

☐ Cambridgeshire
☐ Essex
☐ Lancashire
☐ Yorkshire

10. What is 'Aggers's' full name?

☐ James Agnew
☐ Jonathan Agnew
☐ Jonathan Aggrington
☐ Alan Pardew

ANSWERS

1 Two. 2 Yorkshire. 3. Nottingham. 4 None. 5 W. G. 6 Yorkshire. 7 Stewart. 8 Caught and bowled. 9 Lancashire. 10 Jonathan Agnew.

117

QUIZ 57: 1960s TV

1. Which series featured the characters Emma Peel and Steed?
- ☐ The Avengers
- ☐ The Man From Uncle
- ☐ The New Avengers
- ☐ The New Seekers

2. Where was Cathy told to Come in the 1966 play about home-lessness?
- ☐ Away
- ☐ Down the pub
- ☐ Home
- ☐ Out

3. What was "That was the week that was" abbreviated to?
- ☐ Newsnight
- ☐ TTTWWW
- ☐ TW3
- ☐ That Week

4. What was the nickname of amateur sleuth Simon Templar?
- ☐ The Saint
- ☐ The Sinner
- ☐ Spider-Man
- ☐ Steed

5. Which long-running hymn singing programme began in 1961?
- ☐ Highway
- ☐ Morning Worship
- ☐ My Way
- ☐ Songs of Praise

6. Which series starred the controversial Alf Garnett?

☐ One Foot In the Grave
☐ On the Buses
☐ Steptoe and Son
☐ Till Death Do Us Part

7. Which World about new inventions and discoveries began in 1965?

☐ Future World
☐ New World
☐ The Tomorrow People
☐ Tomorrow's World

8. Which chart music show started in 1964?

☐ Cheggers Plays Pop
☐ Jukebox Jury
☐ Ready Steady Go!
☐ Top of the Pops

9. Who played in the football match watched by 32 million people in 1966?

☐ England, Brazil
☐ England, West Germany
☐ West Germany, Russia
☐ West Germany, Brazil

10. Who starred with Peter Cook in "Not Only… But Also"?

☐ Bo Derek
☐ David Frost
☐ Dudley Moore
☐ Richard Stillgoe

ANSWERS

1 The Avengers. 2 Home. 3 That was the Week That was. 4 The Saint. 5 Songs of Praise. 6 Till Death Do Us Part. 7 Tomorrow's World. 8 Top of the Pops.

119

QUIZ 58: HARRY POTTER

1. Which actor played Hagrid in the Harry Potter films?
- [ ] Robbie Coltrane
- [ ] Billy Connolley
- [ ] Bill Nighy
- [ ] Daniel Radcliffe

2. Which company bought J. K. Rowling's first script and published the novel?
- [ ] André Deutsch
- [ ] Bloomsbury
- [ ] Penguin
- [ ] Random House

3. Cornelius Fudge is the Minister for what?
- [ ] Education
- [ ] Magic
- [ ] Owls
- [ ] Sweets

4. Which city is a favoured venue for midnight launches with J. K. Rowling present?
- [ ] Edinburgh
- [ ] Hogwarts
- [ ] London
- [ ] Paris

5. Which Chris directed the first Harry Potter movie?
- [ ] Carter
- [ ] Columbus
- [ ] Rowling
- [ ] Smith

6. What is the name of the Slytherin Student who keeps company with Draco Malfoy?

- [ ] The Bloody Baron
- [ ] Harry Potter
- [ ] Pansy Parkinson
- [ ] Tom Marvolo Riddle

7. Which character did the late Richard Harris play on film?

- [ ] Aberforth Dumbledore
- [ ] Albus Dumbledore
- [ ] Argus Filch
- [ ] Ariana Dumbledore

8. Parselmouth is the name for a wizard that can do what?

- [ ] Blow things up
- [ ] Talk to cats
- [ ] Talk to dogs
- [ ] Talk to snakes

9. What type of transport appears on the cover of the children's edition of The Philosopher's Stone?

- [ ] Bicycle
- [ ] Bus
- [ ] Car
- [ ] Train

10. What is the name of Ron's pet rat?

- [ ] Harry
- [ ] Hermione
- [ ] Ratty
- [ ] Scabbers

ANSWERS

1 Robbie Coltrane. 2 Bloomsbury. 3 Magic. 4 Edinburgh. 5 Chris Columbus. 6 Pansy Parkinson. 7 Albus Dumbledore. 8 Talk to snakes. 9 Train. 10 Scabbers.

121

QUIZ 59: THE UK

1. On which river does Hull lie?
- ☐ Derwent
- ☐ Humber
- ☐ Tees
- ☐ Tyne

2. Which city's major station is New Street?
- ☐ Birmingham
- ☐ Exeter
- ☐ Liverpool
- ☐ Manchester

3. In which city is Princes Street a major shopping thoroughfare?
- ☐ Bristol
- ☐ Edinburgh
- ☐ Glasgow
- ☐ London

4. On which coast of Scotland is Dundee?
- ☐ North
- ☐ East
- ☐ South
- ☐ West

5. Which motorway would you travel on from London to Cambridge?
- ☐ M1
- ☐ M1A
- ☐ M11
- ☐ M12

6. London Zoo is in which Park?
- ☐ Hyde Park
- ☐ Regent's Park
- ☐ St James Park
- ☐ Zoo Park

7. Which motorway stretches from the outskirts of London into Wales?
- ☐ M1
- ☐ M2
- ☐ M3
- ☐ M4

8. On which island are Shanklin and Sandown?
- ☐ Arran
- ☐ Ireland
- ☐ Isle of Man
- ☐ Isle of Wight

9. Which two south-coast resorts include the name Regis?
- ☐ Bognor, Brine
- ☐ Bognor, Lyme
- ☐ Bognor, Western
- ☐ Lyme, Thyme

10. In which London borough is Stoke Newington?
- ☐ Camden
- ☐ Hackney
- ☐ Haringey
- ☐ Westminster

ANSWERS

1 Humber. 2 Birmingham. 3 Edinburgh. 4 East. 5 M11. 6 Regent's Park. 7 M4. 8 Isle of Wight. 9 Bognor, Lyme. 10 Hackney.

123

QUIZ 60: ELTON JOHN

1. Which 1979 hit was a remixed 2003 No. 1 for Elton?

☐ Are You Ready For Love?

☐ Candle In The Wind

☐ Don't Go Breaking My Heart

☐ Goodbye Yellow Brick Road

2. Who collaborated with Elton on the score of "Aida"?

☐ Andrew Lloyd Webber

☐ Cameron Mackintosh

☐ Tim Rice

☐ Bernie Taupin

3. Which song has the line, "I sat on the roof and kicked off the moss"?

☐ My Song

☐ Saturday Night's Alright For Fighting

☐ The Roof Song

☐ Your Song

4. Elton went through a civil "marriage" ceremony with which long-time partner?

☐ Kiki Dee

☐ David Furnish

☐ Ed Sheeran

☐ Bernie Taupin

5. What was the name of the record label Elton John started?

☐ His Master's Voice

☐ Pocket

☐ Rocket

☐ Virgin

10 "Rocket Man".

6. Elton teamed up with Blue for which No. 1 single?

☐ Are You Ready For Love?
☐ Don't Go Breaking My Heart
☐ Saturday Night's Alright For Fighting
☐ Sorry Seems to be the Hardest Word

7. Which club made an F.A. Cup Final when Elton was Chairman?

☐ Barcelona
☐ QPR
☐ Reading
☐ Watford

8. Who duetted with Elton on the 2002 version of "Your Song"?

☐ Kiki Dee
☐ Paul McCartney
☐ Ewan MacGregor
☐ Alessandro Safina

9. Which controversial artist did Elton partner at the US Grammy 2001 awards?

☐ Eminem
☐ Lady Gaga
☐ Marilyn Manson
☐ Metallica

10. Which song contains the words, "and all this science I don't understand"?

☐ Don't Let The Sun Go Down On Me
☐ I'm Still Standing
☐ Rocket Man
☐ Your Song

ANSWERS

QUIZ 61: ENTERTAINERS

1. What type of pet did Manuel adopt in "Fawlty Towers"?
- [ ] Cat
- [ ] Moose
- [ ] Mouse
- [ ] Rat

2. Which future James Bond starred in "Our Friends in the North"?
- [ ] Pierce Brosnan
- [ ] Daniel Craig
- [ ] Roger Moore
- [ ] David Niven

3. What was Terry's sister called in "The Likely Lads"?
- [ ] Audrey
- [ ] Louise
- [ ] Thelma
- [ ] Simone

4. Which series featured Benny, Judy, Trisha and Tucker when it began?
- [ ] Biker Grove
- [ ] Blue Peter
- [ ] Grange Hill
- [ ] Vision On

5. Who was the third of "Take Three Girls" with Kate and Avril?
- [ ] Caroline
- [ ] Charlene
- [ ] Vanessa
- [ ] Victoria

6. In what type of place was "Waiting for God" set?

- ☐ Heaven
- ☐ Old people's home
- ☐ Police station
- ☐ Psychiatric hospital

7. Who was Jim London in "Up the Elephant and Round the Castle"?

- ☐ Jim Davidson
- ☐ Adam Faith
- ☐ Dudley Moore
- ☐ Freddie Star

8. What relation was Hattie Jacques to Eric in their "Sykes and ..." series?

- ☐ Auntie
- ☐ Cook
- ☐ Mother
- ☐ Sister

9. What did Harold Steptoe always call his father?

- ☐ Daddy
- ☐ Father
- ☐ You dirty old man
- ☐ You naughty old man

10. Which chat show was presented by the "togmeister"?

- ☐ Chris Evans
- ☐ Graham Norton
- ☐ Jon Togg
- ☐ Terry Wogan

—————————————————————————————— ANSWERS

1 Rat. 2 Daniel Craig. 3 Audrey. 4 Grange Hill. 5 Victoria. 6 Old people's home. 7 Jim Davidson. 8 Sister. 9 "You dirty old man". 10 Terry Wogan

Quiz 55: Royals

1. Which Jubilee did the Queen celebrate in 2002?

- ☐ Bronze
- ☐ Silver
- ☐ Golden
- ☐ Diamond

2. In 2002, the Queen lost her mother and which other close relative?

- ☐ Father
- ☐ Sister
- ☐ Brother
- ☐ Twin

3. Which castle was badly damaged by fire in 1992?

- ☐ Balmoral
- ☐ Buckingham
- ☐ Tower of London
- ☐ Windsor

4. What is Prince Harry's proper first name?

- ☐ Henry
- ☐ Harold
- ☐ Harrigbert
- ☐ Harry

5. Which Royal survived a kidnap attempt in 1974?

- ☐ Princess Anne
- ☐ Prince Charles
- ☐ Prince Edward
- ☐ Prince Philip

6. Which son of the Queen has a daughter called Louise?

☐ Andrew
☐ Charles
☐ Edward
☐ Mark

7. Prince Charles is Duke of which county of southwest England?

☐ Cornwall
☐ Devon
☐ Somerset
☐ Wales

8. Which title did Edward VIII take after he abdicated?

☐ Duke of Earl
☐ Duke of Wales
☐ Duke of Windsor
☐ Mr

9. What is the name of the Queen's residence in Norfolk?

☐ Balmoral
☐ Cromer
☐ Sandringham
☐ Norfolk House

10. The Queen's granddaughter Zara Phillips is accomplished in which sport?

☐ Horseriding
☐ Rowing
☐ Shooting
☐ Wrestling

1 Golden Jubilee. 2 Her sister (Princess Margaret). 3 Windsor. 4 Windsor. 5 Princess Anne. 6 Prince Edward. 7 Cornwall. 8 Duke of Windsor. 9 Sandringham. 10 Horseriding.

Quiz 62: Media

1. What does the B in BAFTA stand for?

- [ ] Best
- [ ] Birmingham
- [ ] Borough
- [ ] British

2. Jeremy Isaacs was the first chief executive of which channel?

- [ ] BBC1
- [ ] BBC2
- [ ] ITV
- [ ] Channel 4

3. Which title is given to the chief executive of the BBC?

- [ ] Director General
- [ ] General Director
- [ ] Managing Director
- [ ] Master

4. Which London-based Sunday paper was founded in 1990?

- [ ] Independent on Sunday
- [ ] News of the World
- [ ] Observer
- [ ] Sunday Sport

5. In which town is Red Rose radio based?

- [ ] Peterborough
- [ ] Preston
- [ ] Scarborough
- [ ] York

6. What is the more common name for a teleprompt?

☐ Autocue
☐ Lino
☐ Prompter
☐ Wordscreen

7. Who sets the rate for the television licence?

☐ BBC
☐ EU
☐ Parliament
☐ Prime Minister

8. Which channel has the slogan "Make the voyage"?

☐ The Discovery Channel
☐ The DIY Channel
☐ The Travel Channel
☐ The Voyage Channel

9. In a TV studio what is a dolly?

☐ A cross-dresser
☐ A make-up woman
☐ A mounting for a camera
☐ A mounting for a microphone

10. What is a studio's chief electrician called?

☐ Gaffer
☐ Grip
☐ Sparks
☐ Sparky

1 British. 2 Channel 4. 3 Director General. 4 Independent on Sunday. 5 Preston. 6 Autocue. 7 Parliament. 8 The Discovery Channel. 9 A mounting for a camera. 10 Gaffer.

QUIZ 63: HISTORY

1. Which British monarch succeeded Queen Victoria?
☐ Elizabeth II
☐ Edward VI
☐ Edward VII
☐ George VII

2. Richard III died at which battle?
☐ Bosworth Field
☐ Barnet
☐ Hastings
☐ York

3. Who was the last viceroy of India?
☐ Clive
☐ George VI
☐ Prince Louis of Battenburg
☐ Lord Louis Mountbatten

4. Which English monarch married Eleanor of Aquitaine?
☐ Henry II
☐ Henry IV
☐ Henry VI
☐ Henry VIII

5. Who was the last wife of Henry VIII?
☐ Anne of Cleves
☐ Catherine of Aragon
☐ Catherine Howard
☐ Catherine Parr

6. Which country did Britain fight in the War of Jenkins' Ear?

- [ ] France
- [ ] Ireland
- [ ] Spain
- [ ] Wales

7. Which King George did the Prince Regent become?

- [ ] George IV
- [ ] George III
- [ ] George II
- [ ] George I

8. At the Siege of Mafeking who led the British forces?

- [ ] Robert Baden-Powell
- [ ] Colonel B. T. Mahon
- [ ] Fieldmarshal Bernard Montgomery
- [ ] Louis Mountbatten

9. The House of Lancaster kings were all called what?

- [ ] Charles
- [ ] Edward
- [ ] George
- [ ] Henry

10. Apart from Mad George, which kinder nickname did George III have?

- [ ] Big George
- [ ] Farmer Giles
- [ ] Farmer George
- [ ] Happy George

——————————————————————— ANSWERS

1 Edward VII. 2 Bosworth Field. 3 Lord Louis Mountbatten. 4 Henry II. 5 Catherine Parr. 6 Spain. 7 George IV. 8 Robert Baden-Powell. 9 Henry. 10 Farmer George.

133

QUIZ 64: POLITICS

1. Which prime minister's father was a trapeze artist?

☐ Tony Blair
☐ John Major
☐ John Smith
☐ Margaret Thatcher

2. The House of Commons consists of how many members?

☐ 606
☐ 699
☐ 648
☐ 651

3. Who replaced Alan Clark as MP for Kensington & Chelsea?

☐ Michael Gove
☐ Michael Mann
☐ Michael Meacher
☐ Michael Portillo

4. Who gave up the title of Viscount Stansgate to remain an MP?

☐ Tony Banks
☐ Tony Benn
☐ Hilary Benn
☐ Tony Blair

5. Which MP is the son-in-law of Alf Garnett's son-in-law?

☐ Tony Banks
☐ Tony Benn
☐ Hilary Benn
☐ Tony Blair

6. Who was the leader of the opposition at the time of the 2001 general election?

☐ David Cameron
☐ William Hague
☐ John Major
☐ Ian Duncan Smith

7. What was the first name of the wife of the leader of the opposition in the 2005 general election?

☐ Cherie
☐ Irma
☐ Sam
☐ Sandra

8. Who wrote the novel "A Parliamentary Affair"?

☐ Jeffrey Archer
☐ Tony Blair
☐ Edwina Currie
☐ John Major

9. Who resigned as a gov't minister over the Sara Keays affair?

☐ Geoffrey Howe
☐ Cecil Parkinson
☐ Norman Pym
☐ Norman Tebbit

10. Which party won the general election in 1945?

☐ Conservative
☐ Labour
☐ Liberal
☐ Lib/Dem Alliance

ANSWERS

1 John Major's. 2 651. 3 Michael Portillo. 4 Tony Benn. 5 Tony Blair. 6 William Hague.
7 Sandra. 8 Edwina Currie. 9 Cecil Parkinson. 10 Labour.

QUIZ 65: 1960s

1. George Blake gained notoriety as what?
- ☐ Boxer
- ☐ Chef
- ☐ Policeman
- ☐ Spy

2. Which Francis sailed solo round the world?
- ☐ Bacon
- ☐ Chichester
- ☐ Drake
- ☐ Frost

3. Who was involved with John Lennon in a "bed-in" for peace?
- ☐ Julian Lennon
- ☐ Yoko Ono
- ☐ May Pang
- ☐ Ringo Starr

4. Which President originally blocked Britain's entry into the EEC?
- ☐ Chirac
- ☐ De Gaulle
- ☐ Galtieri
- ☐ Mittérand

5. Which country banned a tour by England's cricketers?
- ☐ Australia
- ☐ Ireland
- ☐ New Zealand
- ☐ South Africa

6. George Brown was a prominent MP for which party?

☐ Conservative
☐ Liberal
☐ Lib/Dem Alliance
☐ Labour

7. Which Private magazine signalled the satire boom?

☐ Private Eye
☐ Private Hole
☐ Private Joke
☐ Private Practice

8. Which theatre that "never closed" finally did close?

☐ Moulin
☐ Noel Coward Theatre
☐ Royal Opera House
☐ Windmill

9. Which Anglo-French supersonic airliner took to the skies?

☐ Concorde
☐ EuroJet
☐ Eurostar
☐ Supermarine Spitfire

10. Who was manager of the Beatles until 1967?

☐ Neil Aspinall
☐ Brian Epstein
☐ Allen Klein
☐ Andrew Loog Oldham

ANSWERS

1 A spy. 2 Chichester. 3 Yoko Ono. 4 De Gaulle. 5 South Africa. 6 Labour.
7 Private Eye. 8 Windmill. 9 Concorde. 10 Brian Epstein.

137

QUIZ 66: BOOKS

1. Who created the Discworld books?
- [ ] Douglas Adams
- [ ] Iain Banks
- [ ] George R. R. Martin
- [ ] Terry Pratchett

2. Which Ian created James Bond?
- [ ] Douglas
- [ ] Fleming
- [ ] McEwan
- [ ] Rankin

3. Which creatures are the central characters in "Watership Down"?
- [ ] Cats
- [ ] Dogs
- [ ] Rabbits
- [ ] Wolves

4. Who wrote "Rebecca"?
- [ ] Agathan Christie
- [ ] Noel Coward
- [ ] Daphne Du Maurier
- [ ] Joan Fontaine

5. What was the name of the boy in "The Jungle Book"?
- [ ] Jai
- [ ] Jim
- [ ] Mowgli
- [ ] Tarzan

6. Which novelist born in 1886 had the initials H. G.?
- ☐ Chesterton
- ☐ Hardy
- ☐ Dickens
- ☐ Wells

7. Which children's publisher has a black & red insect as its logo?
- ☐ Blackbird
- ☐ Ladybird
- ☐ Penguin
- ☐ Puffin

8. Who created Inspector Adam Dalgleish?
- ☐ Agatha Christie
- ☐ P. D. James
- ☐ Ruth Rendell
- ☐ Dorothy L. Sayers

9. Which Douglas wrote "The Hitch Hiker's Guide to the Galaxy"?
- ☐ Douglas Adams
- ☐ Ian Douglas
- ☐ Douglas Rushkoff
- ☐ Louise Douglas

10. Brother Cadfael belonged to which order of monks?
- ☐ Jesuit
- ☐ Carmelite
- ☐ Benedictine
- ☐ Constantine

ANSWERS

1 Terry Pratchett. 2 Fleming. 3 Rabbits. 4 Daphne Du Maurier. 5 Mowgli. 6 Wells 7 Ladybird. 8 P. D. James. 9 Adams. 10 Benedictine.

139

QUIZ 67: HORSE RACES

1. In 1990 Mr Frisk set a record time in which major race?
- ☐ 1,000 Guineas
- ☐ 2,000 Guineas
- ☐ Derby
- ☐ Grand National

2. Which Earl of Derby gave his name to the race?
- ☐ 10th
- ☐ 11th
- ☐ 12th
- ☐ 13th

3. When was Red Rum's third Grand National win?
- ☐ 1976
- ☐ 1977
- ☐ 1978
- ☐ 1979

4. Which jockey rode Best Mate to a hat-trick of Cheltenham Gold Cup wins?
- ☐ Jim Culloty
- ☐ Frankie Dettori
- ☐ Kieren Fallon
- ☐ Lester Piggott

5. Which of these races is not part of the English Triple Crown?
- ☐ 2,000 Guineas
- ☐ Derby
- ☐ Grand National
- ☐ St Leger

6. How did 19th-century jockey Fred Archer die?

☐ Committed suicide
☐ Fell from his horse
☐ Poisoned
☐ Run over by a horse

7. When did Lester Piggott first win the Derby?

☐ 1952
☐ 1953
☐ 1954
☐ 1955

8. Which classic race was sponsored by Gold Seal from 1984–92?

☐ 2,000 Guineas
☐ The Derby
☐ The Grand National
☐ The Oaks

9. Who rode Devon Loch in the sensational 1956 Grand National?

☐ Jeffrey Archer
☐ Ian Fleming
☐ Dick Francis
☐ Lester Piggott

10. What colour was Arkle?

☐ Bay
☐ Brown
☐ Chestnut
☐ Gray

ANSWERS

1 Grand National. 2 12th. 3 1977. 4 Jim Culloty. 5 Grand National. 6 Committed suicide. 7 1954. 8 The Oaks. 9 Dick Francis. 10 Bay.

141

QUIZ 68: ENGLAND

1. In which city is the University of East Anglia?

☐ Colchester
☐ Ipswich
☐ Lowestoft
☐ Norwich

2. Which county is Thomas Hardy associated with?

☐ Dorset
☐ Essex
☐ Sussex
☐ Wessex

3. Which part of Oxford was famous for motor car manufacture?

☐ Cowley
☐ Chipping Norton
☐ Didcot
☐ North

4. Which Devon port has a famous Hoe?

☐ Bristol
☐ Exeter
☐ Plymouth
☐ Southampton

5. Which county is also known as Salop?

☐ Bedfordshire
☐ Cheshire
☐ Salopshire
☐ Shropshire

6. Which Isle has Needles off its west coast?
☐ Arran
☐ Bryher
☐ Isle of Man
☐ Isle of Wight

7. Where would you find the 18th-century Assembly Rooms and Royal Crescent?
☐ Bath
☐ Brighton
☐ Colchester
☐ York

8. Which of these counties does not exist?
☐ North Yorkshire
☐ South Yorkshire
☐ East Yorkshire
☐ West Yorkshire

9. In which town is the shopping complex, the Metro Centre?
☐ Gateshead
☐ Newcastle
☐ South Shields
☐ Sunderland

10. Where would you find the Backs and the Bridge of Sighs?
☐ Cambridge
☐ Durham
☐ Northampton
☐ Oxford

ANSWERS

1 Norwich. 2 Dorset. 3 Cowley. 4 Plymouth. 5 Shropshire. 6 Isle of Wight. 7 Bath. 8 East. 9 Gateshead. 10 Cambridge.

143

QUIZ 69: 1980s

1. Which controversial BBC Falklands film was broadcast in May 1988?
- ☐ Cathy Come Home
- ☐ Tumbledown
- ☐ Christiane F
- ☐ Who Framed Roger Rabbit?

2. In which month was the marriage of Prince Charles and Lady Diana?
- ☐ June
- ☐ July
- ☐ August
- ☐ September

3. The SAS stormed which embassy in Knightsbridge?
- ☐ American
- ☐ Iranian
- ☐ Iraqi
- ☐ Syrian

4. In August 1980 unemployment in Britain reached what figure?
- ☐ 1 million
- ☐ 2 million
- ☐ 3 million
- ☐ 4 million

5. Which Lord prepared a report following the Brixton riots?
- ☐ Jarman
- ☐ Jessup
- ☐ Scarman
- ☐ Soames

6. Whom did Pat Cash beat in the final when he won Wimbledon?

☐ Bjorn Borg
☐ Ivan Lendl
☐ John Macenroe
☐ Fred Perry

7. Who became the first Pope to visit Britain in 400 years?

☐ Benedict
☐ Pious II
☐ John Paul
☐ John Ringo

8. Which charity record was the last to reach No.1 in the 80s?

☐ Bangla Desh
☐ Do They Know It's Christmas
☐ Ferry Cross The Mersea
☐ We Are The World

9. Who were Liverpool's opponents in the FA Cup semi-final Hillsborough disaster?

☐ Everton
☐ Ipswich
☐ Manchester United
☐ Nottingham Forest

10. Who "got on his bike and looked for work"?

☐ Norman Tebbit
☐ Norman Tebbit's father
☐ Norman Tebbit's mother
☐ Norman Tebbit's son

─────────────────────────────────────── ANSWERS

1 Tumbledown. 2 July. 3 Iranian. 4 Two million. 5 Scarman. 6 Ivan Lendl. 7 John Paul 8 "Do They Know It's Christmas?". 9 Nottingham Forest. 10 Norman Tebbit's father.

145

Quiz 70: Food

1. Which pudding is eaten with roast beef?
- [ ] Black
- [ ] Essex
- [ ] Summer
- [ ] Yorkshire

2. Which vegetables can be French, runner or baked?
- [ ] Beans
- [ ] Carrots
- [ ] Peas
- [ ] Potatos

3. What colour is piccalilli?
- [ ] Blue
- [ ] Brown
- [ ] Green
- [ ] Yellow

4. What are fish fingers mainly made of?
- [ ] Chicken
- [ ] Fish
- [ ] Lamb
- [ ] Soya

5. What colour is wholemeal bread?
- [ ] Black
- [ ] Brown
- [ ] Orange
- [ ] White

6. What is Stinking Bishop?

☐ Beer

☐ A cheese

☐ Cider

☐ An old priest

7. Petits pois are small what?

☐ Beans

☐ Cabbages

☐ People

☐ Peas

8. After beer, what is the other main ingredient of shandy?

☐ Creme de menthe

☐ Cider

☐ Lemonade

☐ Water

9. Which Scottish island has 7 working whisky distilleries on it?

☐ Islay

☐ Mull

☐ Skye

☐ Uist

10. Which of the following is NOT a supermarket?

☐ Morrison

☐ Sainsbury's

☐ Teddy's

☐ Tesco

ANSWERS

Quiz 71: Scotland

1. What does the word "loch" mean?
- [ ] Hill
- [ ] Lake
- [ ] Mountain
- [ ] Valley

2. What is Scotland's highest mountain?
- [ ] Ben Lawers
- [ ] Ben Nevis
- [ ] Ben Macdui
- [ ] Sgor an Lochain Uaine

3. Which city gives its name to a rich fruit cake?
- [ ] Aberdeen
- [ ] Dundee
- [ ] Glasgow
- [ ] Victoria

4. Which city shares its name with a city in Australia?
- [ ] Inverness
- [ ] Montrose
- [ ] Perth
- [ ] Sydney

5. Which river in the Borders gives its name to a woollen fabric?
- [ ] Esk
- [ ] Leith
- [ ] Harris
- [ ] Tweed

6. Which sea is to the east of the Scottish mainland?

- [ ] Dover Straight
- [ ] East Sea
- [ ] English Channel
- [ ] North Sea

7. What is a glen?

- [ ] Hill
- [ ] Lake
- [ ] Mountain
- [ ] Valley

8. In which city is Hampden Park Stadium?

- [ ] Aberdeen
- [ ] Dundee
- [ ] Edinburgh
- [ ] Glasgow

9. Which is farthest north?

- [ ] Dundee
- [ ] Dumfries
- [ ] Edinburgh
- [ ] Glasgow

10. Who is Scotland's patron saint?

- [ ] St Andrew
- [ ] St David
- [ ] St George
- [ ] St John

ANSWERS

1 Lake. 2 Ben Nevis. 3 Dundee. 4 Perth. 5 Tweed. 6 North Sea.
7 Valley. 8 Glasgow. 9 Dundee. 10 St Andrew.

149

QUIZ 72: MIXED BAG

1. Who was the longest-reigning British monarch before Victoria?
- ☐ George I
- ☐ George II
- ☐ George III
- ☐ George IV

2. Which ponies were originally used in coal mines?
- ☐ New Forest Pony
- ☐ Shanks's Pony
- ☐ Shetland Pony
- ☐ Welsh Mountain Pony

3. Who was the first post-war British winner of a British Grand Prix?
- ☐ Jack Brabham
- ☐ Nigel Mansell
- ☐ Stirling Moss
- ☐ Jackie Stewart

4. Which was the Old Trafford Test in the 2005 Ashes?
- ☐ First
- ☐ Second
- ☐ Third
- ☐ Fourth

5. Which bird-shooting season runs from October 1 to February 1?
- ☐ Eagle
- ☐ Grouse
- ☐ Pheasant
- ☐ Sparrow

6. What is the name of Andy Capp's wife?

☐ Andina
☐ Fiona
☐ Flo or Florence
☐ Flora

7. Who was the original owner of Today newspaper?

☐ Alastair Campbell
☐ Rupert Murdoch
☐ Tiny Rowlands
☐ Eddie Shah

8. Who wrote the novel "Sharpe's Tiger"?

☐ Jeffrey Archer
☐ Bernard Cornwell
☐ Ian Fleming
☐ Simon Scarrow

9. In which decade of the 20th century was George Harrison born?

☐ 1930s
☐ 1940s
☐ 1950s
☐ 1960s

10. What do G and K stand for in G. K. Chesterton's name?

☐ George Keith
☐ Gilbert Keith
☐ George Klapka
☐ Gerrard Kross

ANSWERS

1 George III. 2 Shetland. 3 Stirling Moss. 4 Third. 5 Pheasant. 6 Flo or Florrie. 7 Eddy Shah. 8 Bernard Cornwell. 9 40s. 10 Gilbert Keith.

151

QUIZ 73: TV

1. Which former triple jump champion presented "Songs of Praise"?
- [ ] Jonathan Edwards
- [ ] Phillips Idowu
- [ ] Colin Jackson
- [ ] Christian Olsson

2. Who was the third Doctor Who?
- [ ] Tom Baker
- [ ] William Hartnell
- [ ] Jon Pertwee
- [ ] Patrick Stewart

3. What was Zoë's job in "May to December"?
- [ ] History teacher
- [ ] PE teacher
- [ ] Policewoman
- [ ] Tailor

4. In "Lovejoy" what was Tinker's surname?
- [ ] Deal
- [ ] Dellboy
- [ ] Ellis
- [ ] Tim

5. What was the name of the first "Morse" sequel?
- [ ] Endeavour
- [ ] Lewis
- [ ] Old Morse
- [ ] Young Morse

6. Where were the first three series of "Animal Hospital" based?

☐ Great Ormond Street Hospital
☐ Harmsworth Hospital
☐ London Zoo
☐ Windsor Safari Park

7. Who drew the animated titles sequence for "Yes Minister"?

☐ Steve Bell
☐ Gerald Scarfe
☐ Ronald Searle
☐ Ralph Steadman

8. What was the job of the heroes of "Common as Muck"?

☐ Butlers
☐ Dustmen
☐ Policemen
☐ Waitors

9. Who was the first Dr Who to play opposite Billie Piper?

☐ Christopher Eccleston
☐ Paul McGann
☐ Matt Smith
☐ David Tennant

10. Which city is "Casualty"'s Holby said to be?

☐ Bath
☐ Bristol
☐ London
☐ York

ANSWERS

1 Jonathan Edwards. 2 Jon Pertwee. 3 PE teacher. 4 Deal. 5 "Lewis". 6 Harmsworth Hospital. 7 Gerald Scarfe. 8 Dustmen. 9 Christopher Eccleston. 10 Bristol.

153

QUIZ 74: POT LUCK

1. Where was Tony Blair when the London bombs exploded on July 7, 2005?
☐ Chequers
☐ Downing Street
☐ Gleneagles
☐ Italy

2. In which year did John Major become Prime Minister?
☐ 1988
☐ 1989
☐ 1990
☐ 1991

3. Which Briton has been F1 World Champion on the most occasions?
☐ Jack Brabham
☐ Nigel Mansell
☐ Stirling Moss
☐ Jackie Stewart

4. Brontophobia is a fear of what?
☐ Dinosaurs
☐ Lightning
☐ Romantic novels
☐ Thunder

5. Which Somerset hill is famed for its Arthurian associations?
☐ Arthur's Mount
☐ Glastonbury Tor
☐ Mt Glasto
☐ Solsbury Hill

6. Which Welsh town became a city in 1969?

☐ Aberystwyth
☐ Cardiff
☐ Holyhead
☐ Swansea

7. Which fruit provides the basis for Cumberland Sauce?

☐ Apple
☐ Banana
☐ Cherry
☐ Redcurrant

8. In which decade is the movie "Vera Drake" set?

☐ 1930s
☐ 1940s
☐ 1950s
☐ 1960s

9. Rangers' Barry Ferguson played in the Premiership for which club?

☐ Arsenal
☐ Blackburn Rovers
☐ Liverpool
☐ Manchester City

10. Who opened the re-created Globe Theatre in 1997?

☐ Tony Blair
☐ Queen Elizabeth II
☐ Mark Rylance
☐ Peter Street

1. Gleneagles, G8 Summit. 2 1990. 3 Jackie Stewart. 4 Thunder. 5 Glastonbury Tor.
6 Swansea. 7 Redcurrant. 8 1950s. 9 Blackburn Rovers. 10 Queen Elizabeth II

QUIZ 75: FOOTBALL

1. Which famous first will always be held by Keith Peacock?

☐ First red card ever

☐ First sending-off in a league game

☐ First substitution in a league game

☐ First yellow card ever

2. Which club did Mark Atkins play for in a Premiership-winning season?

☐ Blackburn Rovers

☐ Chelsea

☐ Manchester City

☐ Newcastle United

3. Which country did Mike England play for?

☐ England

☐ Northern Ireland

☐ Scotland

☐ Wales

4. What are the home colours of Crystal Palace?

☐ Green & white

☐ Yellow & blue

☐ Red & blue

☐ Red & white

5. Which country did Craig Bellamy play for?

☐ England

☐ Northern Ireland

☐ Scotland

☐ Wales

6. Which team had Radford and Kennedy as a strike force?
- [ ] Arsenal
- [ ] Chelsea
- [ ] Charlton
- [ ] Tottenham Hotspur

7. Which club broke the Auld Firm dominance to win the Scottish League Cup in 2004?
- [ ] Heart of Midlothian
- [ ] Hibernian
- [ ] Livingston
- [ ] Queen of the South

8. Michael Carrick joined Spurs from which other London club?
- [ ] Arsenal
- [ ] Brentford
- [ ] Leyton Orient
- [ ] West Ham

9. To two years, when did the late, great George Best leave Man Utd?
- [ ] 1970
- [ ] 1974
- [ ] 1978
- [ ] 1982

10. Who has managed both Southampton and Celtic?
- [ ] Neil Lennon
- [ ] Gary McAllister
- [ ] Tony Mowbray
- [ ] Gordon Strachan

QUIZ 76: 1950s

1. What was the peak of Edmund Hilary's achievements in 1953?
☐ Climbing every Munro in Scotland
☐ Reaching Annapurna's summit
☐ Reaching Everest's base camp
☐ Reaching Everest's summit

2. Which film classification was introduced to show films were unsuitable for the under 16s?
☐ 15 certificate
☐ 16 certificate
☐ AA certificate
☐ X certificate

3. Which character in children's comics was the "Pilot of the Future"?
☐ Algie
☐ Biggles
☐ Dan Dare
☐ Frank Hampson

4. Which Hugh became leader of the Labour Party?
☐ Gaitskell
☐ Jackson
☐ Jarse
☐ Sculley

5. What was a London pea-souper?
☐ Fog
☐ Smog
☐ Smoke
☐ Soup

6. The 1951 Festival of Britain was centred on which city?

- ☐ Bradford
- ☐ Birmingham
- ☐ London
- ☐ Southampton

7. Which radio show featured Bluebottle and Eccles?

- ☐ Dick Barton
- ☐ The Goon Show
- ☐ Hancock's Half Hour
- ☐ ITMA

8. Which Len captained England as they won the Ashes?

- ☐ Cook
- ☐ Gooch
- ☐ Hutton
- ☐ Willis

9. Manchester United's Bobby Charlton survived a plane crash in which city?

- ☐ Berlin
- ☐ Paris
- ☐ Manchester
- ☐ Munich

10. Which Billy became the first English soccer player to win 100 caps?

- ☐ Bunter
- ☐ Briggs
- ☐ Gladwin
- ☐ Wright

ANSWERS

1 Reaching Everest's summit. 2 X certificate. 3 Dan Dare. 4 Gaitskell. 5 Smog. 6 London. 7 'The Goon Show'. 8 Hutton. 9 Munich. . 10 Wright.

159

QUIZ 77: ROYALTY

1. Which Duchess comforted a weeping Jana Novotna at Wimbledon?
☐ Kent
☐ Sussex
☐ Wales
☐ York

2. What was the maiden name of Sophie, Countess of Wessex?
☐ Ellis-Bextor
☐ Rhys-Jones
☐ Rhys-Thomas
☐ Shand

3. What is the Queen's residence in Norfolk called?
☐ Sandhurst
☐ Sandringham
☐ Windsor
☐ Yarmouth

4. Which school did Prince William attend in his teens?
☐ Eton
☐ Harrow
☐ Marlborough
☐ Oxford

5. Who is next in line to the throne after Prince William?
☐ Prince Charles
☐ Prince Harry
☐ Prince Michael
☐ Prince Phillip

6. With which royal did Capt Peter Townsend have a romance?

- [ ] Princess Anne
- [ ] Princess Margaret
- [ ] Queen Elizabeth
- [ ] The Queen Mother

7. What was the name of the king immediately before Elizabeth II?

- [ ] Charles
- [ ] George
- [ ] Henry
- [ ] James

8. Which royal has a daughter called Zara?

- [ ] Princess Anne
- [ ] Prince Charles
- [ ] Princess Margaret
- [ ] Princess Sara

9. Which royal couple organized a large golden-wedding anniversary celebration in 1997?

- [ ] Princess Anne and Captain Mark Phillips
- [ ] Charles and Camilla
- [ ] Charles and Diana
- [ ] The Queen and Prince Philip

10. Which royal highlighted the problem of landmines in Angola?

- [ ] Princess Anne
- [ ] Prince Andrew
- [ ] Prince Charles
- [ ] Princess Diana

ANSWERS

1 Kent. 2 Rhys-Jones. 3 Sandringham. 4 Eton. 5 Prince Harry. 6 Princess Margaret. 7 George (VI). 8 Princess Anne. 9 The Queen and Prince Philip. 10 Diana.

161

QUIZ 78: TV COMEDY

1. Who impersonated Angela Rippon in "Not the Nine O'Clock News"?
- ☐ Rowan Atkinson
- ☐ Griff Rhys-Jones
- ☐ Mel Smith
- ☐ Pamela Stephenson

2. Who closed his show with "May your god go with you"?
- ☐ Dave Allen
- ☐ Jasper Carrott
- ☐ Barry Cryer
- ☐ Dick Emery

3. Who came to fame in "The Comedians" reaching Walford?
- ☐ Frank Carson
- ☐ Alan Ford
- ☐ Mike Reid
- ☐ Pam St Clement

4. Which "Only Fools and Horses" characters were the chief couple in the spinoff "The Green Green Grass"?
- ☐ Boycie and Marlene
- ☐ Bodie and Doyle
- ☐ Boycie and Boycie
- ☐ Brian and Jed

5. Which sitcom featured Jean and Lionel?
- ☐ As Time Goes By
- ☐ Bless This House
- ☐ One Foot in the Grave
- ☐ On the Buses

10 The Kumars at No 42.

6. Who joined French and Saunders in writing "Girls on Top"?

☐ Kathy Burke
☐ Joanna Lumley
☐ Pamela Stephenson
☐ Ruby Wax

7. In "The Frost Report" John Cleese was upper class and Ronnie Barker middle class: who was working class?

☐ Graham Chapman
☐ Ronnie Corbett
☐ Dennis Norden
☐ Bill Oddie

8. In which show would you find "The Argument Clinic" and the game show "Blackmail"?

☐ The Goon Show
☐ ITMA
☐ Monty Python's Flying Circus
☐ Not the 9 o'clock news

9. Which 90s show featured "Jessie's Diets"?

☐ The Fast Show
☐ Naked Video
☐ The Office
☐ The Smell of Reeves & Mortimer

10. In which show did Sanjeev ask celebrities into his home?

☐ The Kumars at No 42
☐ The Kumars at No 101
☐ The Kumar Show
☐ Sanjeev's Show

ANSWERS

1 Pamela Stephenson, 2 Dave Allen, 3 Mike Reid, 4 Boycie and Marlene, 5 As Time Goes By, 6 Ruby Wax, 7 Ronnie Corbett, 8 Monty Python's Flying Circus, 9 The Fast Show.

163

QUIZ 79: SOAPS

1. "Home and Away" is set near which Australian city?
- [ ] Adelaide
- [ ] Darwin
- [ ] Perth
- [ ] Sydney

2. Which soap's 20th anniversary storyline was about a Ramsay Street documentary?
- [ ] Coronation Street
- [ ] Emmerdale
- [ ] Home and Away
- [ ] Neighbours

3. Who is the most senior of the Archer family?
- [ ] Jack
- [ ] John
- [ ] Peggy
- [ ] Phil

4. Which is the only day of the week Radio 4's "The Archers" is broadcast in the morning?
- [ ] Saturday
- [ ] Sunday
- [ ] Monday
- [ ] Tuesday

5. Which soap is set in Erinsborough?
- [ ] Coronation Street
- [ ] Emmerdale
- [ ] Home and Away
- [ ] Neighbours

6. What was the name of Joan Collins's character in "Dynasty"?

- ☐ Alexia
- ☐ Alexis
- ☐ JR
- ☐ Joan

7. Which soap is set in the city that hosted the 2002 Commonwealth Games?

- ☐ The Archers
- ☐ Coronation Street
- ☐ EastEnders
- ☐ Emmerdale

8. Which comic soap was set around the organization of the 2012 Olympic Games?

- ☐ 2012
- ☐ The Games
- ☐ LOCOG
- ☐ Park and Ride

9. Which soap is set in Borsetshire?

- ☐ The Archers
- ☐ Coronation Street
- ☐ EastEnders
- ☐ Emmerdale

10. Which dish is the Rover's Return's Betty Williams famous for?

- ☐ Curry chips
- ☐ Fish and chips
- ☐ Hotpot
- ☐ Spotted dick

ANSWERS

1 Sydney, 2 "Neighbours", 3 Phil, 4 Sunday, 5 "Neighbours", 6 Alexis, 7 "Coronation Street" (Manchester), 8 "2012", 9 "The Archers", 10 Hotpot.

165

QUIZ 92: POLITICS

1. Which minister resigned over findings in the Budd Report?
- [ ] David Blunkett
- [ ] Charles Clarke
- [ ] John Prescott
- [ ] Jack Straw

2. Which ex-Tory politician left prison in 2000?
- [ ] Jonathan Aitken
- [ ] Jeffrey Archer
- [ ] Mary Archer
- [ ] John Grisham

3. Jack Straw was appointed to which post after Labour's victory in 2001?
- [ ] Foreign Secretary
- [ ] Minister for Education
- [ ] Transport Minister
- [ ] Secretary of State

4. What was Mo Mowlam's real first name?
- [ ] Marjorie
- [ ] Maureen
- [ ] Mavis
- [ ] Moe

5. Over which Bill did Tony Blair's Labour government lose their first Commons vote?
- [ ] Education
- [ ] EU membership
- [ ] NHS
- [ ] Terrorism

10 Iain Duncan Smith.

6. Who resigned as Leader of the House in 2003 over Iraq?

☐ Robin Cook
☐ Clare Short
☐ John Smith
☐ Jack Straw

7. Name Tony Blair's youngest Secretary of State for Education?

☐ Charles Clarke
☐ Alan Johnson
☐ Ruth Kelly
☐ Estelle Morris

8. Who replaced the MP for Sheffield Brightside as Secretary of State for Work and Pensions?

☐ David Blunkett
☐ Tony Blair
☐ Peter Hain
☐ John Hutton

9. After the 2005 election Deputy PM John Prescott held which other post?

☐ Deputy Prime Minister
☐ First Secretary of State
☐ Secretary of State for Education
☐ Secretary of State for Work and Pensions

10. Which politician wrote a novel called "The Devil's Tune"?

☐ Jeffry Archer
☐ Kenneth Clarke
☐ Edwina Curry
☐ Iain Duncan Smith

ANSWERS

1 David Blunkett. 2 Jonathan Aitken. 3 Foreign Secretary. 4 Marjorie. 5 Terrorism Bill. 6 Robin Cook. 7 Ruth Kelly. 8 John Hutton. 9 First Secretary of State.

167

QUIZ 80: 1980s TV

1. In which university city was Inspector Morse based?

☐ Bristol
☐ Cambridge
☐ Durham
☐ Oxford

2. In which eastern country was "The Jewel in the Crown" set?

☐ India
☐ Nepal
☐ Pakistan
☐ Thailand

3. Which emergency service is featured in "London's Burning"?

☐ Ambulance
☐ Coastguard
☐ Fire service
☐ Police

4. Which series featured Ian McShane as an antiques dealer?

☐ Acorn Antiques
☐ Antiques Roadshow
☐ Flambards
☐ Lovejoy

5. What wasn't a news bulletin but did feature Pamela Stephenson and Rowan Atkinson?

☐ Alas Smith and Jones
☐ Not the News at 10
☐ Not the 9 O'clock News
☐ Question Time

6. When was the shop with David Jason and Ronnie Barker Open?

- [ ] All Hours
- [ ] Frequently
- [ ] Never
- [ ] On Sundays

7. Who began presenting "This is Your Life" in 1987?

- [ ] Michael Aspel
- [ ] Cilla Black
- [ ] Hughie Green
- [ ] Michael Parkinson

8. Which pets featured on the programmes with Barbara Woodhouse?

- [ ] Cats
- [ ] Dogs
- [ ] Mice
- [ ] Snakes

9. Which Rat revived the flagging fortunes of TV-am?

- [ ] Pat
- [ ] Reggie
- [ ] Roger
- [ ] Roland

10. Which satirical programme featured latex puppets?

- [ ] The Fast Show
- [ ] Football Extra
- [ ] The Muppet Show
- [ ] Spitting Image

————————————————————————— ANSWERS

1 Oxford 2 India 3 Fire Brigade 4 Lovejoy 5 19 Not the Nine o'Clock News 6 All Hours 7 Michael Aspel 8 Dogs 9 Roland 10 Spitting Image

169

Quiz 81: Football

1. What colour are England's home shirts?
☐ Blue
☐ Green
☐ Red
☐ White

2. Tony Parkes was caretaker manager of which Premiership club?
☐ Blackburn
☐ Blackpool
☐ Bolton
☐ West Ham

3. At which Midland club did England striker Darius Vassell begin his career?
☐ Aston Villa
☐ Birmingham
☐ Bolton
☐ Wolverhampton

4. What was Bolton's home ground for most of the 20th century?
☐ The Baseball Ground
☐ Burnden Park
☐ Buxton
☐ The Reebok

5. Vinny Jones has played for which country?
☐ England
☐ Northern Ireland
☐ Scotland
☐ Wales

6. At which club did Alan Shearer start his league playing career?

☐ Blackburn
☐ Bolton
☐ Newcastle
☐ Southampton

7. Who was Celtic's boss when they first won the European Cup?

☐ Alex Ferguson
☐ Neil Lennon
☐ Jimmy McGrory
☐ Jock Stein

8. Which Italian side did Gazza play for?

☐ AS Roma
☐ Fiorentian
☐ Internazionale
☐ Lazio

9. Which club did Alex Ferguson leave to go to Manchester United?

☐ Aberdeen
☐ Dundee
☐ Dundee United
☐ Rangers

10. Which Spurs keeper scored in a 60s Charity Shield game?

☐ Bill Brown
☐ Pat Jennings
☐ Tony Parks
☐ Paul Robinson

———————————————————————————————— ANSWERS
7 Jock Stein. 8 Lazio. 9 Aberdeen. 10 Pat Jennings.
1 White. 2 Blackburn. 3 Aston Villa. 4 Burnden Park. 5 Wales. 6 Southampton.

171

QUIZ 82: THE UK

1. Cumbernauld is near which British city?
- ☐ Cumberland
- ☐ Dumfries
- ☐ Edinburgh
- ☐ Glasgow

2. Which Sea joins the St George's Channel and the North Channel?
- ☐ English Channel
- ☐ Irish Sea
- ☐ North Sea
- ☐ Red Sea

3. In which county is Chequers, the Prime Minister's country residence?
- ☐ Bedfordshire
- ☐ Berkshire
- ☐ Buckinghamshire
- ☐ Surrey

4. What is England's second largest cathedral?
- ☐ Bristol
- ☐ Ripon
- ☐ Southwell
- ☐ York Minster

5. Which Firth lies between south-west Scotland and north-west England?
- ☐ Cromarty Firth
- ☐ Firth of Forth
- ☐ The Fifth Firth
- ☐ Solway Firth

6. Where is The Cathedral Church of St Michael, consecrated in 1962?

☐ Birmingham
☐ Coventry
☐ London
☐ York

7. Which Leicestershire town is famous for its pork pies?

☐ Ashby-de-la-Zouch
☐ Loughbourough
☐ Melton Mowbray
☐ Wigston Magna

8. What are the canals in Cambridge called?

☐ Canals
☐ The Backs
☐ The Fronts
☐ Little rivers

9. In which county is the southern end of the Pennine Way?

☐ Cheshire
☐ Derbyshire
☐ South Yorkshire
☐ Staffordshire

10. Which Roman road shares its name with a type of fur?

☐ Cat Street
☐ Ermine Street
☐ Mink Street
☐ Watling Street

ANSWERS

1 Glasgow. 2 Irish Sea. 3 Buckinghamshire. 4 York Minster. 5 Solway Firth. 6 Coventry. 7 Melton Mowbray. 8 The Backs. 9 Derbyshire. 10 Ermine Street.

173

QUIZ 83: CITIES

1. In which city is Lime Street station and the Albert Dock?
☐ Liverpool
☐ Manchester
☐ Southampton
☐ Taunton

2. On which Channel Island is St Peter Port?
☐ Alderney
☐ Guernsey
☐ Jersey
☐ Sark

3. Which road leads from Trafalgar Square up to Buckingham Palace?
☐ Birdcage Walk
☐ The Mall
☐ Pall Mall
☐ Whitehall

4. St Annes lies to the south of which major seaside resort?
☐ Blackpool
☐ Great Yarmouth
☐ Weston-Super-Mare
☐ Westward Ho

5. Which is the only Scottish region beginning with F?
☐ Fife
☐ Forfar
☐ Forest of Deane
☐ Fylde

6. Which tunnel is a major link around the M25?

- ☐ Blackwall
- ☐ Dartford
- ☐ EuroTunnel
- ☐ M25 Tunnell

7.Which motorway would you travel on from Birmingham to Lancaster?

- ☐ M4
- ☐ M4a
- ☐ M5
- ☐ M6

8. Which county lies between Norfolk and Essex?

- ☐ Cambridgeshire
- ☐ Kent
- ☐ Lincolnshire
- ☐ Suffolk

9. In which city is Sauciehall Street?

- ☐ Cambridge
- ☐ Edinburgh
- ☐ Glasgow
- ☐ Kilmarnock

10. Which part of the country does London's Euston station serve?

- ☐ North
- ☐ East
- ☐ South
- ☐ West

ANSWERS

1 Liverpool. 2 Guernsey 3 The Mall. 4 Blackpool. 5 Fife.
6 Dartford. 7 M6. 8 Suffolk. 9 Glasgow. 10 North.

QUIZ 84: WAYNE ROONEY

1. In which city was Wayne born?

- [ ] Bolton
- [ ] Brighton
- [ ] Liverpool
- [ ] Manchester

2. Rooney scored his first England goal against which country?

- [ ] Albania
- [ ] Greece
- [ ] Macedonia
- [ ] Wales

3. Which Everton manager gave Rooney his debut?

- [ ] Alex Ferguson
- [ ] Roberto Martinez
- [ ] David Moyes
- [ ] Walter Smith

4. In which year was Rooney born?

- [ ] 1983
- [ ] 1984
- [ ] 1985
- [ ] 1986

5. Where did Everton finish in the Premiership in Rooney's first season?

- [ ] 1st
- [ ] 3rd
- [ ] 5th
- [ ] 7th

6. Against which country did Rooney make his England debut?

☐ Australia
☐ Macedonia
☐ Nigeria
☐ Wales

7. Rooney was first sent off against which Premiership side?

☐ Arsenal
☐ Birmingham
☐ Chelsea
☐ Derby County

8. Which BBC award did he win in 2002?

☐ Commentators' Player of the Year
☐ Sportsman of the Year
☐ Sports Personality of the Year
☐ Young Sports Personality of the Year

9. Which squad number did Rooney take at Man. Utd?

☐ 8
☐ 9
☐ 10
☐ 11

10. Which player left Man. Utd to make Rooney's number available?

☐ David Beckham
☐ Nicky Butt
☐ Eric Cantona
☐ Paul Scholes

ANSWERS

1 Liverpool. 2 Macedonia 3 David Moyes. 4 1985. 5 7th. 6 Australia. 7 Birmingham. 8 BBC Young Sportsperson of the Year. 9 Number 8. 10 Nicky Butt

177

QUIZ 85:

1. How would you orally address an Archbishop?
☐ Sir
☐ Sire
☐ Your archship
☐ Your grace

2. Which seaside resort has Squires Gate airport?
☐ Blackpool
☐ Great Yarmouth
☐ Weston-Super-Mare
☐ Westward Ho

3. Which number can be used as an alternative to 999?
☐ 111
☐ 112
☐ 606
☐ 16

4. What is the maximum weight you can send letters at the basic rate?
☐ 50g
☐ 60g
☐ 70g
☐ 80g

5. What colour is a 1p postage stamp?
☐ Black
☐ Blue
☐ Dark red
☐ Light red

COMMUNICATIONS

6. What colour is an airmail sticker?

☐ Black
☐ Blue
☐ Dark red
☐ Light red

7. Which two cities are the termini for the Anglia rail region?

☐ London & Great Yarmouth
☐ London & Ipswich
☐ London & Norwich
☐ London & Paris

8. Which underground line goes to Heathrow Terminals?

☐ Central
☐ Northern
☐ Piccadilly
☐ Victoria

9. What is the UK's oldest Sunday newspaper?

☐ News of the World
☐ Observer
☐ Sunday Sport
☐ Scotland on Sunday

10. What colour is the logo for Virgin trains?

☐ Black
☐ Red and grey
☐ Red and white
☐ White

ANSWERS

1 Your Grace. 2 Blackpool. 3 112. 4 60g. 5 Dark red. 6 Blue. 7 London, Norwich.
8 Piccadilly. 9 The Observer. 10 Red and grey.

179

QUIZ 86: 1970S TV

1. Who was told It Ain't Half Hot in the sit com set in India?

☐ Dad

☐ Mrs

☐ Mum

☐ Wallah

2. When will it be Alright in the Denis Norden series begun in 1977?

☐ In the morning

☐ On the night

☐ The next day

☐ The week after

3. Who "Played Pop"?

☐ Cheggers (Keith Chegwin)

☐ Rolfers (Rolf Harris)

☐ Maggers (Maggie Philbin)

☐ Edders (Noel Edmonds)

4. Which series about three delinquent OAPs began in the 1970s?

☐ Keeping Up Appearances

☐ Last of the Summer Wine

☐ The OAP Delinquents

☐ One Foot in the Grave

5. Whose Flying Circus was a big hit?

☐ John Cleese's

☐ George Grosz's

☐ Monty Python's

☐ Billy Smart's

6. Which early-evening news magazine was transmitted throughout the country?

☐ Nationwide
☐ The One Show
☐ Sixty Minutes
☐ The Today Programme

7. Which series about sheep dog trials began in the 1970s?

☐ Blue Peter
☐ C'mon Shep
☐ Man's Best Friend
☐ One Man and His Dog

8. Which Liverpool shipping Line was an extremely popular long-running series?

☐ Blue Star
☐ Onedin
☐ P and O
☐ White Star

9. In which part of the country was the Poldark series set?

☐ Cornwall
☐ Devon
☐ Kent
☐ London

10. What was the title of the series about Rigsby and Miss Jones?

☐ Bless this House
☐ George and Mildred
☐ Rising Damp
☐ Trouble Next Door

ANSWERS

Quiz 87: Scotland

1. How many bridges are there over the Firth of Forth?
- [ ] 1
- [ ] 2
- [ ] 3
- [ ] 4

2. What lies between Charlotte Square and St Andrew's Square?
- [ ] Prince's Street
- [ ] Princess Street
- [ ] Pudding Lane
- [ ] Queen's Avenue

3. Where was the childhood home of the late Queen Mother?
- [ ] Balmoral
- [ ] Glamis Castle
- [ ] Scone Palace
- [ ] Stirling Castle

4. What is the industrial area in and around Livingston nicknamed?
- [ ] Living Hell
- [ ] Siliconiston
- [ ] Silicon Glen
- [ ] Silicon Valley

5. Which canal links the lochs of the Great Glen?
- [ ] Caledonian Canal
- [ ] Crinan Canal
- [ ] Dingwall Canal
- [ ] Falkirk Wheel

6. Which historic island is off the southwest of the Isle of Mull?
- [ ] Iona
- [ ] Isay
- [ ] Islay
- [ ] Kintyre

7. What is the name of Edinburgh's stadium where the Commonwealth Games have been held?
- [ ] Easter Road
- [ ] Hampden Park
- [ ] Meadowbank
- [ ] Murrayfield

8. Which rail bridge is the longest in Europe?
- [ ] Canon Street
- [ ] Forth
- [ ] Tavy Bridge
- [ ] Tay Bridge

9. Which famous whisky is made at Blair Athol?
- [ ] Balmenach
- [ ] Bell's
- [ ] Brora
- [ ] Whistle's

10. Which baronial castle is the seat of the only British subject allowed to maintain his own private army?
- [ ] Atholl Estate
- [ ] Blair Castle
- [ ] Loch Tummel
- [ ] Scone Palace

ANSWERS

1 Two. 2 Princes Street. 3 Glamis Castle. 4 Silicon Glen. 5 Caledonian Canal. 6 Iona. 7 Meadowbank. 8 Tay Bridge. 9 Bell's. 10 Blair Castle.

183

QUIZ 88: WAR

1. Why were British soldiers called Tommies (for Tommy Atkins)?

☐ Tommy fronted a recruitment campaign

☐ Tommy was a famous soldier who died

☐ Tommy was a famous soldier who deserted

☐ Sample name on recruitment form

2. Which new British military force was established in 1918?

☐ RAF

☐ RFC

☐ SAS

☐ SBS

3. The German attack on which country caused Britain to enter the Second World War?

☐ Czechoslovakia

☐ Denmark

☐ Hungary

☐ Poland

4. Which German word meaning "lightning war" entered the English language?

☐ Anschluss

☐ Blitzkrieg

☐ Bürgerkrieg

☐ Wehrmacht

5. According to the poster what did "Careless Talk" do?

☐ Cause accidents

☐ Cost lives

☐ Lose wars

☐ Waste time

6. What was the nickname of broadcaster William Joyce?

- ☐ Lord Ha Ha
- ☐ Lord Haw Haw
- ☐ Mr England
- ☐ The Voice of Reason

7. According to Churchill he had nothing to offer in 1940 but what?

- ☐ Bananas
- ☐ Blood, muck and brass
- ☐ Blood, sweat and tears
- ☐ Misery

8. Which great evacuation of 1940 was called Operation Dynamo?

- ☐ Dunkirk
- ☐ Flanders
- ☐ Paris
- ☐ Vichy France

9. What was the German air force called?

- ☐ Luftwaffe
- ☐ Schutzstaffe
- ☐ Waffen-ss
- ☐ Wehrmacht

10. What were the Local Defence Volunteers renamed?

- ☐ Dad's Army
- ☐ Home Guard
- ☐ Land Girls
- ☐ Likely Lads

ANSWERS

1 Sample name on recruitment form. 2 RAF. 3 Poland. 4 Blitzkrieg. 5 Costs Lives. 6 Lord Haw Haw. 7 Blood, toil, tears and sweat. 8 Dunkirk. 9 Luftwaffe. 10 Home Guard.

185

QUIZ 89: HISTORY

1. Which English queen married Prince George of Denmark?

☐ Anne
☐ Elizabeth I
☐ Elizabeth II
☐ Victoria

2. Blucher commanded which country's troops at the Battle of Waterloo?

☐ Belgian
☐ English
☐ French
☐ Prussian

3. Queen Elizabeth II's grandfather was which monarch?

☐ George III
☐ George IV
☐ George V
☐ George VI

4. Who was the first Prince of Wales?

☐ Charles I
☐ Ethelred the Red
☐ George I
☐ James I

5. Whose last words are reputed to be, "My neck is very slender"?

☐ Anne Boleyn
☐ Ann of Cleves
☐ Catherine of Aragon
☐ Catherine Parr

6. Which monarch was murdered in Berkeley Castle?

☐ Edward II
☐ Edward VII
☐ George III
☐ Henry V

7. In what year did Edward VIII abdicate?

☐ 1934
☐ 1935
☐ 1936
☐ 1937

8. In Britain, who first held the office that today is known as Prime Minister?

☐ George I
☐ William Pitt
☐ Horace Walpole
☐ Robert Walpole

9. In the 15th century which Duke was drowned in Malmsey wine?

☐ Clarence
☐ Claret
☐ Derby
☐ York

10. Who ruled England between Henry I and Henry II?

☐ Charles
☐ Peter
☐ Simon
☐ Stephen

ANSWERS

1 Queen Anne. 2 Prussia. 3 George V. 4 James I (James VI of Scotland). 5 Anne Boleyn. 6 Edward II. 7 1936. 8 Robert Walpole. 9 Clarence. 24 Stephen.

187

QUIZ 90: POLITICS

1. Who first became prime minister?
☐ Disraeli
☐ Gladstone
☐ Primrose
☐ Russell

2. When did John Major first win Huntingdon?
☐ 1981
☐ 1982
☐ 1983
☐ 1984

3. Who was beaten to the Labour leadership by Michael Foot in 1980?
☐ Hilary Benn
☐ Tony Benn
☐ Denis Healey
☐ Neil Kinnock

4. What was the name of the model in the Jeremy Thorpe affair?
☐ Andrew Newton
☐ Scott Parker
☐ Norman Parkinson
☐ Norman Scott

5. Prime Minister Arthur James Balfour belonged to which party?
☐ Conservative
☐ Labour
☐ Liberal
☐ Monster Raving Loony

6. Dennis Skinner is known as the Beast of where?

- ☐ Balham
- ☐ Bodmin
- ☐ Bolsover
- ☐ Parliament

7. Who followed Crossland as Labour's Foreign Secretary?

- ☐ Roy Jenkins
- ☐ David Owen
- ☐ David Steel
- ☐ Shirley Williams

8. Who said that Gorbachev was "a man we can do business with"?

- ☐ Tony Blair
- ☐ John Major
- ☐ Queen Elizabeth II
- ☐ Margaret Thatcher

9. Who was leader when Labour adopted the red rose symbol?

- ☐ Tony Blair
- ☐ Michael Foot
- ☐ Neil Kinnock
- ☐ John Smith

10. Which politician was responsible for the creation of the police force?

- ☐ Benjamin Disraeli
- ☐ William Gladstone
- ☐ Henry John Temple
- ☐ Robert Peel

ANSWERS

1 Disraeli. 2 1983. 3 Denis Healey. 4 Norman Scott. 5 Conservative. 6 Bolsover. 7 David Owen. 8 Margaret Thatcher. 9 Neil Kinnock. 10 Robert Peel.

189

Quiz 91: Rugby

1. Which Scot was Lions captain for the '93 New Zealand tour?
☐ Jeremy Guscott
☐ Gavin Hastings
☐ Scott Hastings
☐ Chris Paterson

2. How old was Will Carling when he first captained England?
☐ 20
☐ 21
☐ 22
☐ 23

3. Who was top try scorer on the Lions 2005 tour of NZ?
☐ Lawrence Dallaglio
☐ Jason Robinson
☐ Martyn Williams
☐ Shane Williams

4. How many countries had won the expanded Six Nations before Wales?
☐ 1
☐ 2
☐ 3
☐ 4

5. On his return to Union which player said, "It's a challenge I don't particularly need"?
☐ Jonathan Davies
☐ David Jones
☐ Keri Jones
☐ Barrie-Jon Mather

6. Who did not play in 2005 after being named Great Britain league captain?

- ☐ Will Carling
- ☐ Lee Dickson
- ☐ Chris Joynt
- ☐ Paul Sculthorpe

7. Where was Jeremy Guscott born?

- ☐ Bath
- ☐ Bristol
- ☐ Exeter
- ☐ Frome

8. Which stadium hosted the League's 1995 World Cup Final?

- ☐ The Millennium Stadium, Cardiff
- ☐ Parc des Princes
- ☐ Twickenham
- ☐ Wembley

9. Over half of the 1997 Lions squad came from which country?

- ☐ England
- ☐ Ireland
- ☐ Scotland
- ☐ Wales

10. Which team ended Wigan's Challenge Cup record run in the 90s?

- ☐ Bradford Bulls
- ☐ Leeds Rhinos
- ☐ Salford Reds
- ☐ Wakefield Trinity Wildcats

ANSWERS

1 Gavin Hastings. 2 22. 3 Shane Williams. 4 Two (England and France). 5 Davies. 6 Paul Sculthorpe (injured). 7 Bath. 8 Wembley. 9 England. 10 Salford Reds.

191

QUIZ 93: POP ALBUMS

1. What was the Kaiser Chiefs' debut album called?
☐ Employment
☐ Off With Their Heads
☐ Souvenir
☐ Yours Truly, Angry Mob

2. Which group were of a Different Class in 1995?
☐ Blur
☐ Pulp
☐ Rolling Stones
☐ Stone Roses

3. In the 90s, who broke out with "The Great Escape"?
☐ Blur
☐ Pulp
☐ Suede
☐ Paul Weller

4. In the 70s who recorded "Goodbye Yellow Brick Road"?
☐ Billy Joel
☐ Elton John
☐ Paul McCartney
☐ Sweet

5. Which Simply Red album featured "For Your Babies" and "Stars"?
☐ Life
☐ Men and Women
☐ Picture Book
☐ Stars

6. "Rumours" provided over 400 weeks on the album chart for whom?

☐ Eagles
☐ Fleetwood Mac
☐ Led Zeppelin
☐ Rolling Stones

7. What was Definitely the first No. 1 album from Oasis?

☐ Definitely Maybe
☐ Definitely Not
☐ Don't Believe the Truth
☐ (What's The Story) Morning Glory?

8. Which David made a surprise comeback in 2013 with a new album?

☐ Beckham
☐ Bowie
☐ Duchovny
☐ Essex

9. Which label launched 'Now That's What I Call Music'?

☐ Apple
☐ EMI
☐ Universal
☐ Virgin

10. Who recorded 'Wish You Were Here'?

☐ Syd Barrett
☐ Eric Clapton
☐ Pink Floyd
☐ Van Morrisson

ANSWERS

1 Employment. 2 Pulp. 3 Blur. 4 Elton John. 5 Stars. 6 Fleetwood Mac. 7 Definitely Maybe. 8 Bowie. 9 Virgin. 10 Pink Floyd.

193

QUIZ 94: THE BEATLES

1. How many Beatles were still alive when the album "1" first became No 1?

☐ 1
☐ 2
☐ 3
☐ 4

2. What was John Lennon's middle name?

☐ Jack
☐ James
☐ Wilson
☐ Winston

3. Which original Beatle did Ringo Starr replace?

☐ Pete Best
☐ Paul McCartney
☐ Rory Storm
☐ Stuart Sutcliffe

4. What was on the other side of the single "We Can Work It Out"?

☐ A Day in the Life
☐ Day Tripper
☐ Hey Jude
☐ She Loves You

5. Which Beatles song was banned by the BBC because its initials were said to be drug-related?

☐ Eleanor Rigby
☐ Everybody's Got Something to Hide Except Me and My Monkey
☐ Glass Onion
☐ Lucy in the Sky with Diamonds

10 The Quarrymen.

6. What did Brian Epstein manage before the Beatles?

☐ A nightclub
☐ A record store
☐ Helen Shapiro
☐ The Rolling Stones

7. What are John Lennon's two sons called?

☐ John and Paul
☐ Julian and Sean
☐ Pete and Dud
☐ Ringo and Pete

8. How was the double album, "The Beatles", better known?

☐ The Black Album
☐ The Last Album
☐ The Lost Album
☐ The White Album

9. On which show did they make their first national TV appearance?

☐ Juke Box Jury
☐ Nationwide
☐ Ready Steady Go!
☐ Thank Your Lucky Stars

10. Which group did John Lennon form and name after his school in 1956?

☐ Johnny and the Moondogs
☐ The Quarrymen
☐ The Silver Beatles
☐ The Sixth Form

1 Three. 2 Winston. 3 Pete Best. 4 Day Tripper. 5 Lucy in the Sky with Diamonds. 6 A record store. 7 Julian and Sean. 8 The White Album. 9 Thank Your Lucky Stars.

QUIZ 95: UK TV

1. Who were the stars of "A Close Shave"?
☐ French and Saunders
☐ Little and Large
☐ Vic and Bob
☐ Wallace and Gromit

2. Who wrote "The Singing Detective" and "Pennies from Heaven"?
☐ Alan Bleasdale
☐ Melvyn Bragg
☐ Dennis Potter
☐ Colin Welland

3. Which Agatha Christie sleuth was played by Geraldine McEwan?
☐ Father Brown
☐ Miss Marple
☐ Ariadne Oliver
☐ Hercule Poirot

4. Who co-starred with Adam Faith in "Love Hurts"?
☐ Daniela Denby-Ashe
☐ Robert Lindsay
☐ David Suchet
☐ Zoe Wanamaker

5. Who is Anthea Turner's TV presenter sister?
☐ Davina McCall
☐ Millicent Turner
☐ Wendy Turner
☐ Emma Willis

6. Who left "Peak Practice" for "Bliss"?

- [ ] Dr Will Preston
- [ ] Richard Platt
- [ ] Simon Shepherd
- [ ] Kevin Whatley

7. Which female replaced Matthew Kelly as host of "Stars in Their Eyes"?

- [ ] Cat Deeley
- [ ] Jordan
- [ ] Mia Michaels
- [ ] Mary Murphy

8. Who was known as the Green Goddess?

- [ ] Clare Moran
- [ ] Diana Moran
- [ ] Selena Scott
- [ ] Lizzie Webb

9. Who first presented the weather on BBC's "Breakfast Time"?

- [ ] Rory Bremner
- [ ] Michael Fish
- [ ] John Kettley
- [ ] Francis Wilson

10. Who was known as the Galloping Gourmet?

- [ ] Keith Floyd
- [ ] Graham Kerr
- [ ] Jeff Smith
- [ ] Martin Yann

ANSWERS

1 Wallace & Gromit. 2 Dennis Potter. 3 Miss Marple. 4 Zoë Wanamaker. 5 Wendy Turner. 6 Simon Shepherd. 7 Cat Deeley. 8 Diana Moran. 9 Francis Wilson.

197

QUIZ 96: TV TIMES

1. Which "EastEnders" character died on his allotment?
☐ Sid Clarke
☐ Arthur Fowler
☐ Cliff Murray
☐ Den Watts

2. Which country is Rab C. Nesbitt from?
☐ England
☐ Ireland
☐ Scotland
☐ Wales

3. Which former "Opportunity Knocks" presenter died in 1997?
☐ Les Dawson
☐ Hughie Green
☐ Michael Miles
☐ Bob Monkhouse

4. Who always embarked on a long monologue in "The Two Ronnies"?
☐ Ronnie Barker
☐ John Cleese
☐ Ronnie Corbett
☐ The Phantom Raspberry blower

5. What did Denis Neville and Oz say to those they left behind in the North-East in the 80s?
☐ Auf Wiedersehen Pet
☐ Giss a job
☐ Whatever happened to the likely lads?
☐ You're lying

6. "QI" is presented by which Stephen?

☐ Banks
☐ Fry
☐ King
☐ Hawking

7. In which sitcom did Private Secretary Bernard Woolley appear?

☐ The New Statesman
☐ Yes Minister
☐ Yes Prime Minister
☐ Woolley's Way

8. Robert Lindsay starred in a sitcom about "My" what?

☐ Bird
☐ Family
☐ House
☐ Life

9. On which day of the week is "The Antiques Roadshow" on?

☐ Saturday
☐ Sunday
☐ Monday
☐ Friday

10. Des Lynam began presenting which words and numbers quiz in October 2005?

☐ Blankety Blank
☐ Catchphrase
☐ Countdown
☐ Definition

ANSWERS

1 Arthur Fowler. 2 Scotland. 3 Hughie Green. 4 Corbett. 5 Auf Wiedersehen Pet. 6 Fry.
7 "Yes Minister". 8 Family. 9 Sunday. 10 "Countdown".

199

QUIZ 97: FOOTBALL

1. How many different French clubs did Eric Cantona play for before joining Leeds?
- [ ] 4
- [ ] 5
- [ ] 6
- [ ] 7

2. Who were Wigan's first ever opponents in the Premiership?
- [ ] Arsenal
- [ ] Chelsea
- [ ] Tottenham
- [ ] West Bromwich Albion

3. Who did Michael Owen scored his first Newcastle goal against?
- [ ] Arsenal
- [ ] Blackburn
- [ ] Leicester
- [ ] Sunderland

4. What was the last English league club George Best played for?
- [ ] Bournemouth
- [ ] Fulham
- [ ] Manchester United
- [ ] Wigan

5. The world's first artificial pitch was built in which city?
- [ ] Barcelona
- [ ] Houston
- [ ] London
- [ ] Singapore

9 Bradford City, 10 Arsenal (v. Palace Feb. 2005).

6. Who got the last hat-trick against Man. Utd before Blackburn's Bentley in 2006?

☐ Dennis Bailey
☐ Frank Lampard
☐ Wayne Rooney
☐ Alan Smith

7. Which city does the striker Chris Armstrong come from?

☐ Chester
☐ Norwich
☐ Newcastle
☐ Sunderland

8. Who was the first manager to record six FA Cup Final wins?

☐ Alex Ferguson
☐ George Ramsay
☐ Bill Shankley
☐ Arsene Wenger

9. Cec Podd created an appearance record for which club?

☐ Bradford City
☐ Bristol City
☐ Huddersfield
☐ Leeds United

10. Which English club was first to be without a single British player in a squad for a game?

☐ Arsenal
☐ Chelsea
☐ Manchest United
☐ Tottenham Hotspur

ANSWERS

1 Five. 2 Chelsea. 3 Blackburn. 4 Bournemouth. 5 Houston Astrodrome. 6 Dennis Bailey (for QPR, 1992). 7 Newcastle. 8 George Ramsay (all with Aston Villa).

201

QUIZ 98: WALES

1. Which Welsh Bay shares its name with a woollen jacket?
☐ Cardigan
☐ Jumper
☐ Porthmadog
☐ Rhyl

2. Which is the only Welsh county to have a first-class cricket team?
☐ Glamorgan
☐ Merthyr Tydfil
☐ Powys
☐ Wrexham

3. What is the currency of Wales?
☐ Euro
☐ Gallic pound
☐ Pound sterling
☐ Welsh pound

4. Wales has the highest density in the world of which animal?
☐ Chickens
☐ Cows
☐ Foxes
☐ Sheep

5. Which Welsh Secretary challenged John Major for the Tory Party leadership in the summer of 1995?
☐ David Davis
☐ Michael Howard
☐ Peter Lilley
☐ John Redwood

6. Which county is further north?

☐ Cardiff
☐ Clwyd
☐ Gwent
☐ Swansea

7. Which Strait separates Anglesey from the mainland?

☐ Anglesey Alley
☐ St George's Channel
☐ Menai Straight
☐ Welsh Straight

8. Which North Wales university town shares its name with a resort of Northern Ireland?

☐ Bangor
☐ Llandudno
☐ Porthmadog
☐ Windsor Castle

9. The UK's longest river rises in Wales. What is it called?

☐ Clwyd
☐ Conway
☐ Dee
☐ Severn

10. Which town is further south?

☐ Aberystwyth
☐ Cardigan
☐ Llanelli
☐ Swansea

1 Cardigan. 2 Glamorgan. 3 Pound sterling. 5 Sheep. 5 John Redwood.
6 Clwyd. 7 Menai Strait. 8 Bangor. 9 Severn. 10 Swansea.

Quiz 99: Media

1. S4C broadcasts in which minority UK language?

☐ French
☐ Greek
☐ Polish
☐ Welsh

2. On which channel was "Brookside" broadcast?

☐ Channel 4
☐ Channel 5
☐ Discovery Channel
☐ ITV

3. What does the first B stand for in BSkyB?

☐ Brian
☐ Bright
☐ British
☐ Best

4. Which day of the week is the Observer published?

☐ Friday
☐ Saturday
☐ Sunday
☐ Monday

5. In early ITV what was shown in a "natural break"?

☐ Advert
☐ News bulletin
☐ Public service announcement
☐ Weather forecast

6. Which daily UK paper was founded in the 80s and ceased in the 90s?

☐ The Digger
☐ The Sport
☐ The Sun
☐ Today

7. What subject is catered for by the magazine Four Four Two?

☐ Cricket
☐ Football
☐ Horseracing
☐ Snooker

8. On which channel were colour broadcasts first seen in the UK?

☐ BBC1
☐ BBC2
☐ Channel 4
☐ ITV

9. In broadcasting what did LWT stand for?

☐ Let's Watch Television
☐ London Weekend Television
☐ London's Watching Television
☐ Lords Watch Tennis

10. Which 90s breakfast TV station was originally known as Sunrise TV?

☐ The Big Breakfast Channel
☐ GMTV
☐ MTV
☐ TVAM

1 Welsh. 2 Channel 4. 3 British Sky Broadcasting. 4 Sunday. 5 Adverts. 6 Today.
7 Football. 8 BBC 2. 9 London Weekend Television. 10 GMTV.

QUIZ 100: ROYALTY

1. Who had a father called Prince Andrew and has a son called Prince Andrew?

- [ ] Prince Charles
- [ ] King George VI
- [ ] Prince Philip
- [ ] Elizabeth I

2. In which cathedral did Charles and Diana marry?

- [ ] Lincoln
- [ ] St Paul's
- [ ] Westminster
- [ ] York Minster

3. In which decade did Elizabeth II come to the throne?

- [ ] 1940s
- [ ] 1950s
- [ ] 1960s
- [ ] 1970s

4. How many children did she have when she became Queen?

- [ ] 0
- [ ] 1
- [ ] 2
- [ ] 3

5. Whose country home is at Highgrove?

- [ ] Prince Andrew
- [ ] Prince Charles
- [ ] Prince Harry
- [ ] Prince Philip

6. Which birthday did the Queen Mother celebrate in 1996?

☐ 93th
☐ 94th
☐ 95th
☐ 96th

7. Rear Admiral Timothy Laurence is married to which of the Queen's children?

☐ Princess Anne
☐ Princess Beatrice
☐ Princess Margaret
☐ Princess Michael

8. Which of the Queen's children is Earl of Wessex?

☐ Prince Andrew
☐ Prince Charles
☐ Prince Edward
☐ Prince Philip

9. Which Princess is married to Angus Ogilvy?

☐ Alexandra
☐ Beatrice
☐ Eugenie
☐ Margaret

10. What was Lord Mountbatten's first name?

☐ Arthur
☐ Charles
☐ Louis
☐ Xavier

1 Prince Philip. 2 St Paul's. 3 1950s. 4 Two. 5 Prince Charles. 6 96th. 7 Princess Anne.
8 Prince Edward. 9 Alexandra. 10 Louis.

QUIZ 101: GEOGRAPHY

1. What is the highest peak in Scotland after Ben Nevis?
- ☐ Aonach Beag
- ☐ Ben Lawers
- ☐ Ben Macdui
- ☐ Braeriach

2. On which river does Dumfries stand?
- ☐ Manchester
- ☐ Mersea
- ☐ Tweed
- ☐ Tyne

3. Where is the James Clerk Maxwell Telescope?
- ☐ Aberdeen
- ☐ Dumfries
- ☐ Nith
- ☐ John O'Groats

4. Which town has the car index mark AA?
- ☐ Aberdeen
- ☐ Edinburgh
- ☐ Glasgow
- ☐ Kirkcaldy

5. Where is Dyce Airport?
- ☐ Aberdeen
- ☐ Dundee
- ☐ Lewis
- ☐ Skye

6. Which Lough is in the centre of the Sperrin, Antrim and Mourne ranges?

- ☐ Lomond
- ☐ Neagh
- ☐ Ness
- ☐ Shin

7. Where is the National Library of Wales?

- ☐ Aberystwyth
- ☐ Cardiff
- ☐ Fishguard
- ☐ Swansea

8. Which town's football ground is farthest away from any other?

- ☐ Brighton
- ☐ Cardiff
- ☐ Carlisle
- ☐ Exeter

9. In which country is the UK's highest mountain?

- ☐ England
- ☐ Northern Ireland
- ☐ Scotland
- ☐ Wales

10. Which English city has the first Jain temple in the western world?

- ☐ Birmingham
- ☐ Bristol
- ☐ Chelmsford
- ☐ Leicester

ANSWERS

1 Ben Macdui. 2 Manchester. 3 Nith. 4 Edinburgh. 5. Aberdeen. 6 Neagh. 7 Aberystwyth. 8 Carlisle. 9 Scotland. 10 Leicester

209

QUIZ 102: HEAVY METAL

1. Which Australian band recruited an English singer in 1980?
- ☐ AC/DC
- ☐ Cold Chisel
- ☐ INXS
- ☐ Midnight Oil

2. Who recorded "Bark at the Moon"?
- ☐ Black Sabbath
- ☐ Fleetwood Mac
- ☐ Johnny and the Moondogs
- ☐ Ozzy Ozbourne

3. What instrument did Ian Paice play?
- ☐ Drums
- ☐ Guitar
- ☐ Keyboards
- ☐ Triangle

4. Which folk singer sang on Led Zep's "The Battle of Evermore"?
- ☐ Sandy Denny
- ☐ Ewan MacColl
- ☐ Kirsty MacColl
- ☐ Shane MacGowan

5. "Smoke on the Water" came from which album?
- ☐ Deep Purple
- ☐ Machine Head
- ☐ Shades of Deep Purple
- ☐ Stormbringer

6. Terry Butler changed his group's name to Black Sabbath after reading a novel by which author?

☐ Jeffrey Archer
☐ Aleister Crowley
☐ Terence Fisher
☐ Dennis Wheatley

7. What instrument does Iron Maiden founder Steve Harris play?

☐ Drums
☐ Guitar
☐ Bass guitar
☐ Saxophone

8. "Naked Thunder" was the first solo album by which singer?

☐ Ian Gillan
☐ Jimmy Page
☐ Ian Paice
☐ Robert Plant

9. Who wrote "Stairway to Heaven"?

☐ John Bonham
☐ Jimmy Page
☐ John Paul Jones
☐ Robert Plant

10. What did Def Leppard drummer Rick Allen lose in a car accident?

☐ Arm
☐ Foot
☐ Hand
☐ Leg

————————————————————————— ANSWERS

1 AC/DC. 2 Ozzy Ozbourne. 3 Drums. 4 Sandy Denny. 5 Machine Head. 6 Dennis Wheatley. 7 Bass guitar. 8 Ian Gillan. 9 Jimmy Page. 10 An arm.

211

QUIZ 103: POT LUCK

1. In which county was there a £59 million robbery in February 2006?

☐ Essex
☐ Greater London
☐ Greater Manchester
☐ Kent

2. What is Cambridge's county-class cricket ground called?

☐ Denny's
☐ Fenner's
☐ University Cricket Club
☐ University Cricket Ground

3. Which Milton Keynes theatre is named after a politician who was also a famous politician's wife?

☐ Nye Bevan
☐ Patricia Hollis
☐ James Lee
☐ Jennie Lee

4. How many bridges span the Tyne at Newcastle?

☐ 1
☐ 2
☐ 5
☐ 10

5. What was Scotland's capital in the 11th–15th centuries?

☐ Aberdeen
☐ Edinburgh
☐ Glasgow
☐ Perth

6. Where is Pontefract racecourse?

☐ Bedstone
☐ Manchester
☐ Wakefield
☐ Weston-super-Mare

7. What is the longest river in Wales?

☐ Taff
☐ Teifi
☐ Towy
☐ Usk

8. On which river does Winchester stand?

☐ Dene
☐ Itchen
☐ Quaggy
☐ Win

9. On which tube line is London's longest tunnel?

☐ Central
☐ Circle
☐ Northern
☐ Victoria

10. Which is farther north?

☐ Barnsley
☐ Halifax
☐ Huddersfield
☐ Leeds

ANSWERS

1 Kent. 2 Fenner's. 3 Jennie Lee. 4 Ten. 5 Perth. 6 Wakefield. 7 Towy. 8 Itchen. 9 Northern. 10 Leeds.

213

QUIZ 104: GEOGRAPHY

1. Where is Jurby Ronaldsway airport?
- [ ] King's Lynn
- [ ] Isle of Wight
- [ ] Isle of Man
- [ ] Llandudno

2. Where is the University College of North Wales?
- [ ] Bangor
- [ ] Cardiff
- [ ] Twywn
- [ ] Swansea

3. Which town has a Theatre Royal and a Gardner Centre?
- [ ] Brighton
- [ ] Bristol
- [ ] Ipswich
- [ ] Norwich

4. What is Bolton's theatre called?
- [ ] Corn Exchange
- [ ] Octagon
- [ ] Royal
- [ ] Windmill

5. Where is Queen of the South Football Club?
- [ ] Aberdeen
- [ ] Dumfries
- [ ] Edinburgh
- [ ] Queensborough

6. Which of these is not a university in Edinburgh?

☐ Edinburgh
☐ Heriot-Watt
☐ Napier
☐ Nevison

7. Which is farther east, Middlesbrough or York?

☐ Middlesbrough
☐ Pontefract
☐ Sheffield
☐ York

8. What is Oxford's county-class cricket ground called?

☐ The Fenters
☐ The Oxford Ground
☐ The Parks
☐ Fenton's

9. Where is the Royal and Ancient Golf Club?

☐ St Andrews
☐ St James
☐ London
☐ Louth

10. On which river does Colchester stand?

☐ Colne
☐ Longford
☐ Ouse
☐ Stour

ANSWERS

6 Nevison. 7 York. 8 The Parks. 9 St Andrews. 10 Colne.
1 Douglas, Isle of Man. 2 Bangor. 3 Brighton. 4 The Octagon. 5 Dumfries.

215

Quiz 105: Politics

1. Which former minister has presented "Six O Six" on Radio 5 Live?
☐ DJ Spoony
☐ Richard Littlejohn
☐ John Major
☐ David Mellor

2. Name the 1992 Tory party chairman who lost his Bath seat?
☐ George Entwhistle
☐ Norman Fowler
☐ Chris Huhne
☐ Chris Patten

3. Which former deputy Labour leader, whose father was once a Catholic priest, stood down after the 1992 General Election?
☐ Tony Benn
☐ Roy Hattersley
☐ Denis Healy
☐ Neil Kinnock

4. What was Norman Tebbitt's job before entering Parliament?
☐ Airline pilot
☐ Hypnotist
☐ Policeman
☐ Soldier

5. Which party did Screaming Lord Sutch represent?
☐ All Night
☐ Conservative
☐ Crazy
☐ Monster Raving Loony

6. Who became deputy Labour leader after the 1992 General Election?

☐ Margaret Beckett
☐ Tony Benn
☐ Neil Kinnock
☐ John Prescott

7. Which constituency did the late Mo Mowlam represent?

☐ Reading East
☐ Reading West
☐ Redcar
☐ Redditch

8. What did the Ecology Party change its name to in 1985?

☐ Eco Party
☐ Green Party
☐ Natural Law Party
☐ Naturalist

9. What was Dennis Skinner's job before he entered Parliament?

☐ Bouncer
☐ Cheese maker
☐ Ice-cream Salesman
☐ Miner

10. Which MP won gold medals at the 1980 and 1984 Olympics?

☐ Sebastian Coe
☐ Steve Cram
☐ Steve Ovett
☐ Daley Thompson

1 David Mellor. 2 Chris Patten. 3 Roy Hattersley. 4 Airline pilot. 5 Monster Raving Loony. 6 Margaret Beckett. 7 Redcar. 8 Green Party. 9 Miner. 10 Sebastian Coe.

QUIZ 106: MEDIA

1. Which was the first British newspaper to issue a colour supplement?
☐ Guardian
☐ Sunday Times
☐ Sunday Sport
☐ Today

2. In comics what was Black Bob?
☐ Car
☐ Horse
☐ Plastic bag
☐ Sheepdog

3. Which daily publication is Britain's oldest?
☐ Daily Record
☐ Lloyd's List
☐ Sporting Life
☐ Times

4. Where is the Western Mail based?
☐ Bristol
☐ Cardiff
☐ Plymouth
☐ Taunton

5. How many Sky channels were there originally in 1989?
☐ 1
☐ 2
☐ 3
☐ 4

6. Which TV technician is responsible for hardware such as props, cranes etc.?

☐ Best boy
☐ Gaffer
☐ Grip
☐ Hand

7. Which newspaper did the Sun replace in 1964?

☐ Daily Herald
☐ Daily Post
☐ Evening Life
☐ Sunday Sun

8. Which UK paper has issues published in Frankfurt and New York?

☐ Financial Times
☐ Guardian
☐ Independent
☐ New York Herald Tribune

9. Which publication, founded in 1868, consists wholly of adverts?

☐ Ebay Gazette
☐ Exchange and Mart
☐ Loot
☐ Vogue

10. What is Liverpool's own regional daily paper called?

☐ Liverpool Echo
☐ Liverpool Times
☐ Merseyside Gazette
☐ News of the Echo

ANSWERS

1 Sunday Times. 2 Sheepdog. 3 Lloyd's List. 4 Cardiff. 5 Four. 6 Grip. 7 Daily Herald. 8 Financial Times. 9 Exchange and Mart. 10 Liverpool Echo.

219

QUIZ 107: HARRY POTTER

1. In "The Half-Blood Prince", Harry is in which year at Hogwarts?
- ☐ 3rd
- ☐ 4th
- ☐ 5th
- ☐ 6th

2. What was the second book to be published?
- ☐ Chamber of Secrets
- ☐ Deathly Hallows
- ☐ Goblet Of Fire
- ☐ Philosopher's Stone

3. Which book has Ron inviting Harry to the Quidditch World Cup?
- ☐ Chamber of Secrets
- ☐ Deathly Hallows
- ☐ Goblet Of Fire
- ☐ Philosopher's Stone

4. Which university did J. K. Rowling attend?
- ☐ Edinburgh
- ☐ Exeter
- ☐ Hogwarts
- ☐ Plymouth

5. What did "DA" stand for?
- ☐ Derwent's Army
- ☐ Dumbledore's Arm
- ☐ Dumbledore's Army
- ☐ Dursley's Aunt

10 Killed (by Lord Voldemont).

6. What is the name of the soul-sucking guards from Azkaban?

☐ Boggarts
☐ Dementors
☐ Ghosts
☐ Weasleys

7. Which Mike directed the movie The Goblet of Fire?

☐ Figgis
☐ Newell
☐ Myers
☐ Smith

8. What is the name of the national wizarding newspaper?

☐ The Daily Prophet
☐ The Fly-nantial Times
☐ The Moon
☐ Wizard!

9. Which book cover depicts a creature rising above some flames?

☐ Chamber of Secrets
☐ Goblet Of Fire
☐ Order of the Phoenix
☐ Philosopher's Stone

10. What has happened to Harry's parents?

☐ Abducted by aliens
☐ Cryogenically frozen
☐ Disappeared
☐ Killed

ANSWERS

1 6th. 2 Chamber Of Secrets. 3 Goblet Of Fire. 4 Exeter. 5 Dumbledore's Army.
6 Dementors. 7 Mike Newell. 8 The Daily Prophet. 9 Order Of The Phoenix.

221

QUIZ 108: PUBS

1. On which famous course is the Sulby Glen Hotel?

☐ 18th hole at St Andrews

☐ Brands Hatch

☐ Epsom

☐ Isle of Man TT race course

2. What is the name of the tiny pub in Bury St Edmunds?

☐ The Clamshell

☐ The Nutshell

☐ The Shoebox

☐ The Tight Fit

3. What was the previous name of the "Merry Harrier" in Devon which gave it the shortest pub name in the country?

☐ W

☐ X

☐ Y

☐ Z

4. What's the name of the bar in Galway Racecourse, which is 210 feet long?

☐ Great Bar-rier Reef

☐ Galway Racecourse Bar

☐ Grand Sand Bar

☐ Grand Stand Bar

5. What is said to be the oldest pub in Northern Ireland?

☐ The Duke of York

☐ Grace Neill's Bar

☐ The Ponderosa

☐ Laverys

10 Crown Liquor Saloon.

6. Which pub in St Albans is an 11th-century building?

☐ The Fighting Cocks

☐ The Old Queen's Head

☐ The Queen's Head

☐ The Spread Eagle

7. In which county is the elevated Tan Hill Inn?

☐ East Yorkshire

☐ North Yorkshire

☐ South Yorkshire

☐ West Yorkshire

8. Which pub in Southwark is mentioned in "Little Dorrit"?

☐ The Dickens

☐ The George Inn

☐ The King George

☐ The Queen's Head

9. Which pub in Drury Street, Glasgow, has one of the longest bars in Britain?

☐ The Art School

☐ The Flying Duck

☐ King Tut's Wah Wah Hut

☐ The Old Horseshoe

10. Which Belfast pub in Great Victoria Street is owned by the National Trust?

☐ Crown Liquor Saloon

☐ King Tut's Wah Wah Hut

☐ New Saloon

☐ Old Liquor Saloon

ANSWERS

1 Isle of Man TT course. 2 The Nutshell. 3 X. 4 Grand Stand Bar. 5 Grace Neill's Bar. 6 The Fighting Cocks. 7 North Yorkshire. 8 The George Inn. 9 The Old Horseshoe.

223

QUIZ 109: 1980s

1. What did Prince Edward re-sign?
- [ ] His allegiance to the crown
- [ ] His commission in the Royal Marines
- [ ] His divorce papers
- [ ] His name on a cheque that bounced

2. Which Tory MP Keith was involved in dodgy applications for shares?
- [ ] Beast
- [ ] Beat
- [ ] Best
- [ ] Brest

3. In which month of 1982 did Argentine forces invade the Falkland Islands?
- [ ] March
- [ ] April
- [ ] May
- [ ] June

4. Protests were based at Greenham Common in which county?
- [ ] Berkshire
- [ ] Buckinghamshire
- [ ] Essex
- [ ] Kent

5. Which police officer was shot outside the Libyan embassy?
- [ ] Keith Blakelock
- [ ] Yvonne Fletcher
- [ ] Geoffrey Fox
- [ ] Keith Maddison

6. What did Monday, October 19, 1987 become known as?

- ☐ Black Monday
- ☐ Blue Monday
- ☐ Crash Monday
- ☐ D-day

7. Which North Sea oil rig exploded with the loss of over 150 lives?

- ☐ Gassi Touil
- ☐ Ixtoc I
- ☐ Piper Alpha
- ☐ Piper Bravo

8. Which former M15 man wrote "Spycatcher"?

- ☐ Roger Hollis
- ☐ Stella Rimington
- ☐ Ian Wright
- ☐ Peter Wright

9. Which crazed gunman committed the Hungerford atrocities?

- ☐ Derrick Bird
- ☐ Eric Borel
- ☐ Thomas Hamilton
- ☐ Michael Ryan

10. In which month was Michael Fish embarrassed by the gales of '87?

- ☐ August
- ☐ September
- ☐ October
- ☐ November

ANSWERS

1 Commission in the Royal Marines. 2 Best. 3 April. 4 Berkshire. 5 Yvonne Fletcher. 6 Black Monday. 7 Piper Alpha. 8 Peter Wright. 9 Michael Ryan. 10 October.

225

QUIZ 110: THE ROLLING

1. What was the name of the 2003 world tour?

☐ 40 Licks

☐ Big Licks

☐ Bridges to Babylon

☐ Steel Wheels

2. Who wrote their first Top Twenty hit?

☐ Holland, Dozier, Holland

☐ Jagger and Richards

☐ Lennon and McCartney

☐ Bernie Taupin

3. Which was their first No 1 to be written by Jagger and Richards?

☐ The First Time

☐ The Last Time

☐ Get off of My Cloud

☐ (I Can't Get No) Satisfaction

4. In which blues band did both Mick Jagger and Charlie Watts perform?

☐ The Animals

☐ Alexis Korner's

☐ Quarrymen

☐ Yardbirds

5. Which album features "Mother's Little Helper"?

☐ Aftermath

☐ Beggars Banquet

☐ Between the Buttons

☐ Their Satanic Majesties Request

6. Which instrument did Brian Jones play, other than guitar, on "Their Satanic Majesties Request"?

☐ Bass guitar
☐ Drums
☐ Sitar
☐ Saxophone

7. How did Brian Jones die?

☐ Drowned in swimming pool
☐ Electrocuted
☐ Jumped off cliff
☐ Run over by bus

8. Which French director made The Stones film "One Plus One"?

☐ Jean-Luc Godard
☐ Eric Rohmer
☐ Martin Scorsese
☐ Francois Truffaut

9. Which Australian outlaw did Mick Jagger play on film?

☐ Paul Hogan
☐ Ned Kelly
☐ Mark "Chopper" Read
☐ Josey Wales

10. What is the name of Mick Jagger's daughter by his first wife, Bianca?

☐ Agger
☐ Jade
☐ Jasmine
☐ Jude

ANSWERS

1 40 Licks. 2 Lennon and McCartney. 3 The Last Time. 4 Alexis Korner's. 5 Aftermath. 6 Sitar. 7 Drowned in pool. 8 Jean-Luc Godard. 9 Ned Kelly. 10 Jade.

227

QUIZ 111: MOVIES

1. Which actor from 2005's "The Magic Roundabout" was born in Burnley?
☐ Jim Broadbent
☐ Sir Ian McKellen
☐ Kylie Minogue
☐ Bill Nighy

2. For which film did Katharine Hepburn win the first best actress BAFTA?
☐ The African Queen
☐ On Golden Pond
☐ Guess Who's Coming To Dinner?
☐ The Lion in Winter

3. In "Love Actually" what is the name of Rowan Atkinson's salesman?
☐ Rasta
☐ Roger
☐ Romeo
☐ Rufus

4. Who played opposite Dirk Bogarde in "Doctor at Sea"?
☐ Brigitte Bardot
☐ Jane Birkin
☐ Catherine Deneuve
☐ Joan Sims

5. Who directed "Four Weddings and a Funeral"?
☐ Chris Columbus
☐ Mike Figgis
☐ Mike Newell
☐ Mike Read

9 Prime of Miss Jean Brodie. 10 Don't Lose Your Head

6. Which Ealing comedy was based on "Noblesse Oblige"?

☐ Kind Hearts and Coronets
☐ The Ladykillers
☐ The Man in the White Suit
☐ Passport to Pimlico

7. Which 1984 film was based on "The Death and Life of Dith Pran"?

☐ 1984
☐ Karate Kid
☐ Killing Fields
☐ Revenge of the Nerds

8. Who was the most prolific writer of "Carry On" scripts?

☐ Peter Butterworth
☐ Peter Rogers
☐ Talbot Rothwell
☐ Gerald Thomas

9. In which film did Maggie Smith call her girls "The crème de la crème"?

☐ Calendar Girls
☐ Oh What A Lovely War
☐ The Prime of Miss Jean Brodie
☐ Travels With My Aunt

10. Which Carry On film was (very) loosely based on the Scarlet Pimpernel?

☐ Carry on Cleo
☐ Carry on Up the Khyber
☐ Don't Lose Your Head
☐ Follow That Camel

ANSWERS

1 Sir Ian McKellen. 2 Lion in Winter. 3 Rufus. 4 Brigitte Bardot. 5 Mike Newell. 6 Kind Hearts and Coronets. 7 Killing Fields. 8 Talbot Rothwell.

229

QUIZ 112: THE UK

1. What is ERNIE's original home town?

☐ Fleetwood
☐ Hartlepool
☐ Lytham St Annes
☐ Whitby

2. What is the high-security prison on the Isle of Wight called?

☐ Belmarsh
☐ Full Sutton
☐ Inverness
☐ Parkhurst

3. In which London Square is the US Embassy?

☐ Berkeley Square
☐ Grosvenor Square
☐ Hanover Square
☐ Portman Square

4. Which disaster does London's Monument commemorate?

☐ 9/11 attack on World Trade Center
☐ Great Fire of London
☐ The Plague
☐ World War II bombings

5. Which waterway divides the Isle of Wight from the mainland?

☐ Firth of Forth
☐ Pentland Firth
☐ Solent
☐ Strait of Dover

6. Which castle has St George's Chapel?

☐ Balmoral

☐ Buckingham Palace

☐ Gleneagles

☐ Windsor

7. What is the nearest seaside resort to London?

☐ Blackpool

☐ Clacton-on-Sea

☐ Southend

☐ Southampton

8. Where in London are there gates named after Margaret Thatcher?

☐ Downing Street

☐ House of Commons

☐ House of Lords

☐ St Paul's Cathedral

9. Which theatre was founded in 1959 at Blackfriars in London?

☐ Barbican

☐ Mermaid

☐ The Noel Coward Theatre

☐ Windmill

10. Dogger Bank is off which English county?

☐ Northumberland

☐ Essex

☐ Greater Manchester

☐ Tyne and Wear

ANSWERS

1 Lytham St Annes. 2 Parkhurst. 3 Grosvenor Square. 4 Great Fire of London. 5 The Solent. 6 Windsor. 7 Southend. 8 Downing Street. 9 Mermaid. 10 Northumberland.

231

QUIZ 113: ENTERTAINERS

1. What was the Richard O'Sullivan spin-off from "Man About the House"?

☐ George and Mildred
☐ Robin's Nest
☐ Three's A Crowd
☐ Women About the House

2. Daphne Manners and Hari Kumar were characters in which series?

☐ Bleak House
☐ Brideshead Revisited
☐ The Jewel in the Crown
☐ Tandoori Nights

3. Jimmy Jewel & Hylda Baker were Eli & Nellie Pledge in which show?

☐ For The Love Of Ada
☐ Love Thy Neighbour
☐ Nearest and Dearest
☐ Not On Your Nellie

4. Which veteran actress played the wife in "Meet the Wife"?

☐ Jane Freeman
☐ Thora Hird
☐ Glenda Jackson
☐ Maggie Smith

5. In which classic did you find Blanco, Lukewarm and Gay Gordon?

☐ Boys From the Blackstuff
☐ Only Fools and Horses
☐ Porridge
☐ The Singing Detective

6. What was Bernard Hedges's nickname in "Please Sir"?

☐ Bernie

☐ Hedgey

☐ Hedgehog

☐ Privet

7. What was the surname of George and Mildred?

☐ Best

☐ Clark

☐ Roper

☐ Smith

8. Which flatmates originally lived in Huskisson Road, Liverpool?

☐ Boys From the Blackstuff

☐ Buckingham Palace

☐ The Likely Lads

☐ The Liver Birds

9. What make of car did Nurse Emmanuel drive in "Open All Hours"?

☐ Mini

☐ Morris Minor

☐ Morris Oxford

☐ It was a bicycle

10. In which show did Reg Varney play Stan Butler?

☐ Man About the House

☐ On the Buses

☐ The Rag Trade

☐ Steptoe and Son

ANSWERS

1 "Robin's Nest", 2 "The Jewel in the Crown", 3 "Nearest and Dearest", 4 Thora Hird, 5 "Porridge", 6 Privet, 7 Roper, 8 "The Liver Birds", 9 Morris Minor, 10 "On the Buses".

233

QUIZ 114: ENGLAND

1. Which English county has the longest coastline?
- [ ] Cornwall
- [ ] Essex
- [ ] Kent
- [ ] Norwich

2. Who is responsible for the blue plaques in London?
- [ ] The Blue Plaque Trust
- [ ] English Heritage
- [ ] National Trust
- [ ] Parliament

3. In which London borough are there the most blue plaques?
- [ ] Camden
- [ ] City of London
- [ ] Hackney
- [ ] Westminster

4. What was Marble Arch originally designed to be?
- [ ] Bus shelter
- [ ] Gateway to Buckingham Palace
- [ ] A homage to L'arc de triomphe in Paris
- [ ] Monument to the forgotten soldier

5. What is the stately home owned by the Spencer family in Northamptonshire called?
- [ ] Althorp
- [ ] Holdenby House
- [ ] Rockingham Castle
- [ ] Sandringham House

10 Bedford.

6. Where are Grimes Graves?

- [ ] Essex
- [ ] London
- [ ] Norfolk
- [ ] Suffolk

7. Where is England's largest castle?

- [ ] Cumbria
- [ ] Leeds
- [ ] London
- [ ] Windsor

8. Which two English cathedrals have three spires each?

- [ ] Bristol and Derby
- [ ] Lichfield and Truro
- [ ] Southwell and York Minster
- [ ] St Paul's and Oxford

9. Which county used to be divided into Parts?

- [ ] North Lincolnshire
- [ ] North East Lincolnshire
- [ ] Leicestershire
- [ ] Lincolnshire

10. Which dukes are associated with Woburn Abbey?

- [ ] Bedford
- [ ] Cornwall
- [ ] Devonshire
- [ ] Earl

ANSWERS

1 Cornwall. 2 English Heritage. 3 Westminster. 4 Gateway to Buckingham Palace. 5 Althorp. 6 Norfolk. 7 Windsor. 8 Lichfield and Truro. 9 Lincolnshire.

235

QUIZ 115: AUSTEN

1. What was the occupation of Jane Austen's father?
- [ ] Clergyman
- [ ] Judge
- [ ] Policeman
- [ ] Writer

2. Which Austen novel was originally called "First Impressions"?
- [ ] Emma
- [ ] Mansfield Park
- [ ] Pride and Prejudice
- [ ] Sense and Sensibility

3. Whom does Emma take under her wing in the novel of the same name?
- [ ] Miss Bates
- [ ] Jane Fairfax
- [ ] George Knightley
- [ ] Harriet Smith

4. Which Austen novel was first called "Elinor and Marianne"?
- [ ] Emma
- [ ] Mansfield Park
- [ ] Northanger Abbey
- [ ] Sense and Sensibility

5. Who played Elizabeth Bennet in TV's "Pride and Prejudice" in 1995?
- [ ] Jennifer Ehle
- [ ] Susannah Harker
- [ ] Polly Maberly
- [ ] Julia Sawalha

Thompson. 10 Charlotte.

6. Which of these is not in "Persuasion"?

☐ Anne Elliot
☐ Elizabeth Elliot
☐ Emma Elliott
☐ Mary Elliot

7. In "Mansfield Park" what is the name of the heroine?

☐ Francis Price
☐ Fanny Price
☐ Fanny Prideaux
☐ Fanny Pride

8. In which Austen novel do we meet Catherine Morland?

☐ Emma
☐ Mansfield Park
☐ Northanger Abbey
☐ Sense and Sensibility

9. Who wrote the screenplay for "Sense and Sensibility"?

☐ Kenneth Branagh
☐ Hugh Grant
☐ Kelly Macdonald
☐ Emma Thompson

10. Of the Brontë sisters that survived to adulthood who was the eldest?

☐ Anne
☐ Charlotte
☐ Emily
☐ Emma

ANSWERS

1 Clergyman. 2 Pride and Prejudice. 3 Harriet Smith. 4 Sense and Sensibility. 5 Jennifer Ehle. 6 Emma. 7 Fanny Price. 8 Northanger Abbey. 9 Emma

QUIZ 116: CHAPLIN

1. In which part of London did Chaplin spend his early life?
- [ ] East Ham
- [ ] Hackney
- [ ] Lambeth
- [ ] West Ham

2. What was his elder brother and fellow performer called?
- [ ] Craig
- [ ] David
- [ ] George
- [ ] Sydney

3. What did the troupe, the Eight Lancashire Lads, do?
- [ ] Clog dancing
- [ ] Juggling
- [ ] Tumbling
- [ ] Wrestling

4. With which company did Chaplin travel to the US in 1910?
- [ ] Eight Lancashire Lads
- [ ] Fred Karno
- [ ] Stan Laurel
- [ ] Frederick John Westcott

5. For which company did Chaplin make his first films?
- [ ] Cineville
- [ ] Fox
- [ ] Keystone
- [ ] Mutual Film Corporation

6. Who played the title role in "The Kid" in 1921?

- ☐ John Astin
- ☐ Ted Cassidy
- ☐ Jackie Coogan
- ☐ Carolyn Jones

7. Which film appeared in 1925 and had sound added in 1942?

- ☐ City Lights
- ☐ The Gold Rush
- ☐ The Great Dictator
- ☐ Modern Times

8. Which wife of Chaplin co-starred in "Modern Times"?

- ☐ Paulette Goddard
- ☐ Lita Grey
- ☐ Mildred Harris
- ☐ Norma Shearer

9. How many times did Chaplin marry altogether?

- ☐ 3
- ☐ 4
- ☐ 5
- ☐ 6

10. Which was Chaplin's first sound film?

- ☐ The Great Dictator
- ☐ Limelight
- ☐ Modern Times
- ☐ Monsieur Verdoux

1 Lambeth. 2 Sydney. 3 Clog dancing. 4 Fred Karno. 5 Keystone. 6 Jackie Coogan. 7 The Gold Rush. 8 Paulette Goddard. 9 Four. 10 The Great Dictator.

QUIZ 117: TV HISTORY

1. Which Alan Bleasdale show won the BAFTA Drama award in 1982?
- ☐ Boys From the Blackstuff
- ☐ GBH
- ☐ The Monocled Mutineer
- ☐ Our Friends in the North

2. Which character was killed in episode 2 of "Spooks"?
- ☐ Helen Flynn
- ☐ Jed Kelley
- ☐ Tom Quinn
- ☐ Sam Walker

3. Which TV personality ended his show in a white E-type Jag?
- ☐ Simon Dee
- ☐ Bob Mills
- ☐ Tony Blackburn
- ☐ Johnnie Walker

4. Which Alan Plater TV adaptation starred Kenneth Branagh as Guy Pringle?
- ☐ Alfresco
- ☐ Fortunes of War
- ☐ I, Claudius
- ☐ Tutti Frutti

5. Where did Ken Barlow's father get the money that enabled him to move out of Coronation Street?
- ☐ Bank robbery
- ☐ Found it in the Rovers Return
- ☐ Lottery win
- ☐ Premium bond win

6. Who played Josephine opposite Ernie Wise's Napoleon?

☐ Glenda Jackson

☐ Lynn Redgrave

☐ Vanessa Redgrave

☐ Valerie Singleton

7. Who is the richest person to have a bit-part on "Bread"?

☐ Richard Branson

☐ Queen Elizabeth II

☐ Paul McCartney

☐ Ringo Starr

8. Which Eastender thought his father was Pete Beale when it was Kenny?

☐ Cindy Beale

☐ Mark Fowler

☐ David Wicks

☐ Simon Wicks

9. What was Robin Tripp studying when he lived upstairs from the Ropers?

☐ Catering

☐ Dancing

☐ Drawing

☐ Law

10. Who was Sid's next-door neighbour in "Bless This House"?

☐ Jane

☐ Jean

☐ Mike

☐ Trevor

ANSWERS

1 Boys from the Blackstuff. 2 Helen Flynn. 3 Simon Dee. 4 Fortunes of War. 5 A Premium Bond win. 6 Vanessa Redgrave. 7 Paul McCartney. 8 Simon Wicks. 9 Catering.

QUIZ 118: DICKENS

1. In "A Tale of Two Cities" what is the occupation of Sydney Carton?
- [ ] Barrister
- [ ] Binman
- [ ] Postman
- [ ] Solicitor

2. In "Nicholas Nickleby" who is Ralph Nickleby's clerk?
- [ ] Dilbert Bloggs
- [ ] Fred Bloggs
- [ ] Rob Newman
- [ ] Newman Noggs

3. Which of his novels did Dickens say he liked the best?
- [ ] A Tale of Two Cities
- [ ] Charles In Charge
- [ ] David Copperfield
- [ ] Little Dorrit

4. In Oliver Twist's burgling expedition with Bill Sikes what sort of injury does Oliver receive?
- [ ] Broken arm
- [ ] Gunshot wound
- [ ] Sprained wrist
- [ ] Twisted ankle

5. Which historical events are the background to "Barnaby Rudge"?
- [ ] Boer War
- [ ] French Revolution
- [ ] Gordon Riots
- [ ] Ice Age

10 Philip Pirrip.

6. Who are David Copperfield's two vastly different school-friends?

☐ Newman and Baddiel
☐ Proctor and Davies
☐ Steerage and Tiddles
☐ Steerforth and Traddles

7. Which court case is at the heart of "Bleak House"?

☐ Deadlock v Deadlock
☐ Jarndyce v Bleaker
☐ Jarndyce v Jarndyce
☐ Kramer v Kramer

8. In "Hard Times" who is Mr Bounderby's housekeeper?

☐ Mrs Cleanit
☐ Mrs Gradgrind
☐ Mrs Malaprop
☐ Mrs Sparsit

9. In "Little Dorrit" who are Amy's brother and sister?

☐ Fanny and Alexander
☐ Fanny and Tip
☐ Franny and Pip
☐ Jack and John

10. In "Great Expectations" what is Pip's full name?

☐ Toodle Pip
☐ Paul Pirrip
☐ Pip Pirrip
☐ Philip Pirrip

QUIZ 119: THE BEATLES

1. Whom did the Beatles support on their first nationwide tour?
- ☐ Adam Faith
- ☐ Georgie Fame
- ☐ The Rolling Stones
- ☐ Helen Shapiro

2. Which of these is not a Beatles song?
- ☐ Penny Lane
- ☐ Strawberry Fields
- ☐ Take Me Back
- ☐ The Long and Winding Road

3. On the Royal Variety Show John Lennon invited those in the cheaper seats to clap. What did he tell those in the more expensive seats to do?
- ☐ Drink champagne
- ☐ Leave the theatre
- ☐ Rattle their jewellery
- ☐ Throw money

4. Which Beatle died in Hamburg in 1962?
- ☐ Neil Aspinall
- ☐ Pete Best
- ☐ Rory Storm
- ☐ Stuart Sutcliffe

5. Which solo instrument did John Lennon play on "Love Me Do"?
- ☐ Harmonica
- ☐ Sitar
- ☐ Spoons
- ☐ Xylophone

9 Fred Lennon (John's long-absent father). 10 Parlophone.

6. How many Beatles appeared on one "Juke Box Jury" in 1963?

- [ ] 1
- [ ] 2
- [ ] 3
- [ ] 4

7. What was George Harrison's first solo hit?

- [ ] I Dig Love
- [ ] My Sweet Lord
- [ ] Sing One For The Lord
- [ ] Tandoori Chicken

8. On which show were the Beatles watched by 73 million in the US?

- [ ] The Dean Martin Show
- [ ] The Ed Sullivan Show
- [ ] The Elvis Show
- [ ] Soul Train

9. Who made a record called "That's My Life" in 1965?

- [ ] The Beatles
- [ ] Fred Lennon
- [ ] Julian Lennon
- [ ] Linda McCartney

10. What was the first label the Beatles recorded on with George Martin?

- [ ] Apple
- [ ] EMI
- [ ] Parlophone
- [ ] Virgin

ANSWERS

1 Helen Shapiro. 2 Take Me Back. 3 Rattle their jewellery. 4 Stuart Sutcliffe. 5 Harmonica. 6 All four. 7 My Sweet Lord. 8 The Ed Sullivan Show.

245

QUIZ 120: KIDS TV

1. Who delivers letters in Greendale?
☐ Bob the Builder
☐ Cliff Calvin
☐ Fireman Sam
☐ Postman Pat

2. Which Tank Engine is blue and has the number 1 on it?
☐ Edward
☐ Henry
☐ James
☐ Thomas

3. Wendy, Dizzy and Scoop help which cartoon handyman?
☐ Barney
☐ Bob the Builder
☐ Fireman Sam
☐ Postman Pat

4. Whose vocabulary was limited to words like "flobbalot"?
☐ Andy Pandy
☐ Ant and Dec
☐ Bill and Ben the Flowerpot Men
☐ The Woodentops

5. Whose friends were Teddy and Looby Loo?
☐ Andy Pandy
☐ Bill and Ben
☐ Rag, Tag and Bobtail
☐ The Woodentops

10 "The Wombles".

6. Which show awarded cabbages to its losers?

- [ ] Are You Smarter Than A 10-year-old?
- [ ] Cabbages and Kings
- [ ] Child's Play
- [ ] Crackerjack

7. Which school did Tucker, Zammo and Tegs attend?

- [ ] Brookside Comp
- [ ] Byker Grove
- [ ] Grange Hill
- [ ] Hogwarts

8. Which country did Ivor the Engine come from?

- [ ] England
- [ ] Northern Ireland
- [ ] Scotland
- [ ] Wales

9. Who lives in Fimble Valley?

- [ ] Chorlton
- [ ] The Fimbles
- [ ] Postman Pat
- [ ] Roly Mo

10. In which show did Uncle Bulgaria, Tomsk and Tobermory appear?

- [ ] Balamory
- [ ] Fimbles
- [ ] Tweenies
- [ ] The Wombles

ANSWERS

1 "Postman Pat", 2 Thomas, 3 "Bob the Builder", 4 Bill and Ben the Flowerpot Men, 5 Andy Pandy, 6 "Crackerjack", 7 Grange Hill, 8 Wales, 9 "The Fimbles".

247

QUIZ 121: POLITICIANS

1. Who was the first Tory leader to have gone to a grammar school?

- [ ] Andrew Bonar Law
- [ ] Ted Heath
- [ ] John Major
- [ ] Margaret Thatcher

2. Who was acting leader of the Lib Dems after Charles Kennedy stood down?

- [ ] Alan Beith
- [ ] Vincent Cable
- [ ] Sir Menzies Campbell
- [ ] Paddy Ashdown

3. In 1997 David Blunkett won which constituency?

- [ ] Hillsbrough
- [ ] Sheffield
- [ ] Sheffield Brightside
- [ ] Sheffield Brightside and Hillsbrough

4. What was the name of Harold Wilson's wife?

- [ ] Karen
- [ ] Kate
- [ ] Marie
- [ ] Mary

5. Who published the white paper "In Place of Strife"?

- [ ] Barbara Castle
- [ ] Roy Castle
- [ ] Nigel Cole
- [ ] Harold Wilson

6. Mrs Thatcher became Baroness Thatcher of where?

☐ Downing Street
☐ Duke Street
☐ Kesteven
☐ Lincolnshire

7. In 2004, which former PM's child was linked in a plot involving a military coup?

☐ Brian Major
☐ Carol Thatcher
☐ Dennis Thatcher
☐ Mark Thatcher

8. Who was deputy PM when Harold Macmillan resigned?

☐ Adam Butler
☐ Rab Butler
☐ Anthony Eden
☐ Selwyn Lloyd

9. Tony Blair had how many children when he became Prime Minister?

☐ 1
☐ 2
☐ 3
☐ 4

10. Name the Tory slogan on posters of a queue of the unemployed?

☐ Are you thinking what we're thinking?
☐ Don't trust Labour
☐ Labour isn't working
☐ Queues are for losers like Labour

ANSWERS

1 Ted Heath. 2 Sir Menzies Campbell. 3 Sheffield Brightside. 4 Mary. 5 Barbara Castle.
6 Kesteven. 7 Mark Thatcher. 8 Rab Butler. 9 Three. 10 Labour isn't working.

249

QUIZ 122: UK TV

1. Who became resident cook on GMTV in spring 1997?
- [ ] Ross Burden
- [ ] Paul Rankin
- [ ] Tony Tobin
- [ ] Brian Turner

2. Who first presented "The Antiques Roadshow" in 1981?
- [ ] Michael Aspel
- [ ] Arthur Negis
- [ ] Bruce Parker
- [ ] Hugh Scully

3. Who first presented Channel 4's game show "Deal or No Deal"?
- [ ] Tony Blackburn
- [ ] Keith Chegwin
- [ ] Noel Edmonds
- [ ] Maggie Philbin

4. Who hosted the retrospective quiz show "Backdate"?
- [ ] Cilla Black
- [ ] Julian Clary
- [ ] Paul Merton
- [ ] Valerie Singleton

5. Which star was flown in from the US to introduce the Spice Girls' first live UK performance?
- [ ] Jennifer Aniston
- [ ] Jodie Foster
- [ ] Madonna
- [ ] Ruby Wax

6. Who is dubbed the King of Swing during election campaigns?

☐ David Dimbleby
☐ Dan Snow
☐ Jon Snow
☐ Peter Snow

7. Who replaced Anthea Turner on GMTV's breakfast couch?

☐ Kate Garraway
☐ Lorraine Kelly
☐ Mr Motivator
☐ Fiona Phillips

8. Who is Beverley Callard's actress daughter?

☐ Rebecca Callard
☐ Myanna Buring
☐ Branka Katic
☐ Julia St. John

9. Who first presented "Nine O'Clock Live" on GMTV?

☐ Kate Garraway
☐ Christine Bleakley
☐ Lorraine Kelly
☐ Fiona Phillips

10. Who first presented "Sunday AM", which replaced "Breakfast with Frost"?

☐ David Frost
☐ Eddie Mair
☐ Andrew Marr
☐ Jeremy Paxman

ANSWERS

1 Ross Burden. 2 Hugh Scully. 3 Noel Edmonds. 4 Valerie Singleton. 5 Jennifer Aniston. 6 Peter Snow. 7 Fiona Phillips. 8 Rebecca Callard. 9 Lorraine Kelly. 10 Andrew Marr.

251

QUIZ 123: SCOTLAND

1. What is the most famous cave on Staffa?

☐ Deep Cave
☐ Fingal's Cave
☐ Smuggler's Cave
☐ Smaug's Cave

2. Which palace was once the site of a famous coronation stone?

☐ Culross Palace
☐ Holyrood Palace
☐ Palace of Monimail
☐ Scone Palace

3. Which loch contains the largest volume of fresh water in the British Isles?

☐ Loch Lomond
☐ Loch Morar
☐ Loch Ness
☐ Loch Tay

4. Which city is often called the Fair City?

☐ Brightlingsea
☐ Edinburgh
☐ Perth
☐ Stirling

5. Leanach Farmhouse can be seen on which moorland field of battle?

☐ Bannockburn
☐ Berwick-upon-Tweed
☐ Culloden
☐ Glen Trool

6. On which river does Balmoral stand?

- [ ] Bogie
- [ ] Dee
- [ ] Deveron
- [ ] Don

7. Remains of what type of building are at Kelso and Jedburgh?

- [ ] Abbeys
- [ ] Castles
- [ ] Hairdressers
- [ ] Stables

8. What type of village can be seen at Skara Brae?

- [ ] Ice Age
- [ ] Iron Age
- [ ] Queens of the Stone Age
- [ ] Stone Age

9. Which loch is the largest stretch of inland water in Britain?

- [ ] Loch Lomond
- [ ] Loch Morar
- [ ] Loch Ness
- [ ] Loch Tay

10. Where is Scotland's largest malt whisky distillery?

- [ ] Tomatin
- [ ] Tomintoul
- [ ] Tormore
- [ ] Tullibardine

ANSWERS

1 Fingal's Cave. 2 Scone Palace. 3 Loch Ness. 4 Perth. 5 Culloden. 6 Dee. 7 Abbeys. 8 Stone Age. 9 Loch Lomond. 10 Tomatin.

253

Quiz 124: England

1. Alphabetically what is the last county?
- ☐ West Midlands
- ☐ West Yorkshire
- ☐ Wessex
- ☐ Worcestershire

2. In which Metropolitan county are Trafford and Tameside?
- ☐ Greater Manchester
- ☐ West Midlands
- ☐ West Yorkshire
- ☐ Merseaside

3. In which National Park is Scafell Pike?
- ☐ Brecon Beacons
- ☐ Cumbria
- ☐ Lake District
- ☐ Peak District

4. On which bank of the Thames is the City of London?
- ☐ North
- ☐ East
- ☐ South
- ☐ West

5. In which town is the modernist De La Warr Pavilion to be found?
- ☐ Bexhill-on-Sea
- ☐ Bexleyheath
- ☐ Brighton
- ☐ Lewes

6. Which city is served by John Lennon Airport?

☐ Leeds
☐ Liverpool
☐ Manchester
☐ New York

7. Which county lies between the North Sea and Greater London?

☐ East Sussex
☐ Essex
☐ Kent
☐ Suffolk

8. What is Lindisfarne also known as?

☐ Anglesey
☐ Holy Island
☐ Holy Palace
☐ Unholy Island

9. In which county is Hadrian's Wall?

☐ County Durham
☐ Derby
☐ Northumberland
☐ Scotland

10. From which London station are there trains direct to the continent through the Channel Tunnel?

☐ Kings Cross St Pancras
☐ Liverpool Street
☐ Victoria
☐ Waterloo

ANSWERS

1 Worcestershire. 2 Greater Manchester. 3 Lake District. 4 North. 5 Bexhill-on-Sea. 6 Liverpool. 7 Essex. 8 Holy Island. 9 Northumberland. 10 Kings Cross./St Pancras.

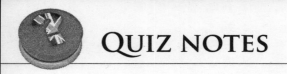

QUIZ NOTES